PRAISE FOR

In the Camps

"While structural racism in the context of Chinese
settler colonialism in Xinjiang evokes similar racisms in
different parts of the world, Darren Byler documents and
analyzes how the new, digitized racialization of China's
Muslim minorities—an 'automated racialization' in a vast
system of internment camps—has taken the meaning of
dehumanization to a completely different level. Stark and
devastating, and yet filled with empathetic detail for the
victims, this book is required reading for anyone interested
in racial justice across the world. Byler's book shows us that
this is not just China's reality but a global reality, where the
violence of one colonial regime cannot be disaggregated
from global complicity."

—SHU-MEI SHIH,
President, American Comparative Literature Association,
and Edward W. Said Professor of Comparative Literature, UCLA

"It's true, no matter how much the Chinese government
denies it—in this richly sourced book, Darren Byler describes
not only how members of Muslim ethnic groups in China
are thrown into re-education camps just for practicing their
religion but also how those outside the camps are deprived of
their freedom by a web of electronic and human surveillance.
Built around true personal stories, the book is a riveting—and
terrifying—account of one of the worst human rights abuses
being perpetrated in the world today."

—ANDREW J. NATHAN,
Class of 1919 Professor of Political Science,
Columbia University

In the Camps
China's High-Tech
Penal Colony

COLUMBIA GLOBAL REPORTS
NEW YORK

In the Camps
China's High-Tech Penal Colony

Darren Byler

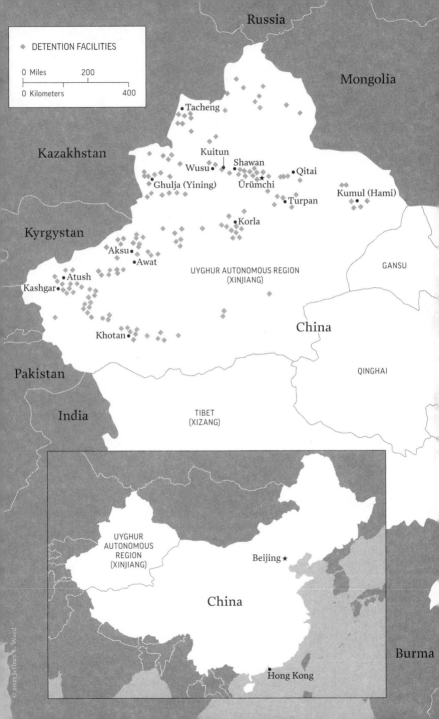

DETENTION FACILITIES

0 Miles   200
0 Kilometers   400

Russia

Mongolia

Kazakhstan

Tacheng

Kuitun
Wusu
Shawan
Qitai
Ghulja (Yining)
Ürümchi
Kumul (Hami)
Turpan

Kyrgystan

Korla

Aksu
Awat
UYGHUR AUTONOMOUS
REGION
(XINJIANG)
GANSU

Atush

Kashgar

China

QINGHAI

Pakistan

India

Khotan

TIBET
(XIZANG)

UYGHUR
AUTONOMOUS
REGION
(XINJIANG)

Beijing ★

China

Burma

Hong Kong

In the Camps
China's High-Tech Penal Colony
Copyright © 2021 by Darren Byler

Published by Columbia Global Reports
91 Claremont Avenue, Suite 515
New York, NY 10027
globalreports.columbia.edu
facebook.com/columbiaglobalreports
@columbiaGR

Library of Congress Cataloging-in-Publication Data
Names: Byler, Darren, author.
Title: In the camps : China's high-tech penal colony / Darren Byler.
Description: New York, NY : Columbia Global Reports, [2021] | Includes
    bibliographical references.
Identifiers: LCCN 2021017638 (print) | LCCN 2021017639 (ebook) | ISBN
    9781735913629 (paperback) | ISBN 9781735913636 (ebook) Subjects: LCSH:
    Internment camps--China. | Penal colonies--China. | Uighur (Turkic people)--
    China--Social conditions. | Electronic surveillance--China.
Classification: LCC HV8964.C5 B95 2021 (print) | LCC HV8964.C5 (ebook) | DDC
    365/.4508994323051--dc23
LC record available at https://lccn.loc.gov/2021017638
LC ebook record available at https://lccn.loc.gov/2021017639

Book design by Strick&Williams
Map design by Jeffrey L. Ward
Author photograph by Darren Byler

Printed in the United States of America

CONTENTS

Introduction

Sometime in mid-2019, a police contractor tapped a young college student from the University of Washington on the shoulder as she walked through a crowded market intersection. The student, Vera Zhou, didn't notice the tapping at first because she was listening to music through her earbuds as she weaved through the crowd. When she turned around and saw the black uniform of a police assistant, the blood drained from her face even as the music kept playing. Speaking in Chinese, Vera's native language, the police officer motioned her into a nearby People's Convenience Police Station—one of more than 7,700 such surveillance hubs that now dot the region.

On a monitor in the boxy gray building, she saw her face surrounded by a yellow square. On other screens she saw pedestrians walking through the market, their faces surrounded by green squares. Beside the high definition video still of her face, her personal data appeared in a black text box. It said that she was Hui, a member of a Chinese Muslim group that makes up around 1 million of the population of 15 million Muslims in

Northwest China. The alarm had gone off because she had walked beyond the parameters of the policing grid of her neighborhood confinement. As a former detainee in a reeducation camp, she was not officially permitted to travel to other areas of town without explicit permission from both her neighborhood watch unit and the Public Security Bureau. The yellow square around her face on the screen indicated that she had once again been deemed a "pre-criminal" by the digital enclosure system that held Muslims in place. Vera said at that moment she felt as though she could hardly breathe. She remembered that her father had told her, "If they check your ID, you will be detained again. You are not like a normal person anymore. You are now one of 'those' people."

Vera was in Kuitun, a small city of around 285,000 in Tacheng Prefecture, an area that surrounds the wealthy oil city of Karamay, and forms the Chinese border with Kazakhstan. She had been trapped there since 2017 when, in the middle of her junior year as a geography student at the University of Washington (where I was an instructor), she had taken a spur-of-the-moment trip back home to see her boyfriend. Her ordeal began after a night at a movie theater in the regional capital Ürümchi, a city of 3.5 million several hours from her home, when her boyfriend received a call asking him to come to a local police station. At the station, the police told him they needed to question his girlfriend. They said they had discovered some suspicious activity in Vera's internet usage. She had used a virtual private network, or VPN, in order to access "illegal websites," such as her university Gmail account. This, they told her later, was a "sign of religious extremism."

It took some time for what was happening to dawn on Vera. Perhaps since her boyfriend was a non-Muslim from the

12 majority Han group and they did not want him to make a scene, at first the police were quite indirect about what would happen next. They just told her she had to wait in the station. When she asked if she was under arrest, they refused to respond. "Just have a seat," they told her. By this time she was quite frightened, so she called her father back in her hometown and told him what was happening. Eventually, a police van pulled up to the station. Four officers piled out, three of them middle aged and one just a teenager, around the same age as Vera. On the sleeve of his uniform, it said "assistant police," the term given for more than ninety thousand private security contractors hired by the police as outsourced labor during the reeducation campaign.

When the officers said they needed to take Vera back to Kuitun to question her, her boyfriend asked quickly if he could drive her back. Maintaining Han-to-Han decorum, the officers said politely that they would need to follow procedures and take her in the van, but that he could follow behind in his car if he liked. She was placed in the back of the van, and once her boyfriend was out of sight, the police shackled her hands behind her back tightly and shoved her roughly into the back seat. The young police contractor, the one who was about the same age as her, was assigned to watch her in the back seat. He sat with one knee splayed to the side at the other end of the bench seat, staring at her blankly, unsmiling, like she was a potential terrorist. She had been put in her place, identified as a Muslim extremist undeserving of civil and human rights.

The region of Xinjiang is located in the northwesternmost corner of China, far into Central Asia and north of another Chinese autonomous region, Tibet. Xinjiang is about the size of

Alaska and borders eight nations, from India to Mongolia. Several groups of Central Asian people are indigenous to the region, the largest of which are the Uyghurs, a Turkic Muslim minority of around 12 million, followed by 1.5 million Kazakhs, 200,000 Kyrgyz, and 15,000 Uzbeks. Han Chinese number about 9 million. In fact, Xinjiang, which simply means "New Frontier" in Chinese, is officially the Xinjiang Uyghur Autonomous Region—an administrative distinction established by the Chinese state that implied a measure of self-rule for Uyghurs.

The Uyghurs have practiced small-scale irrigated farming for centuries in the desert oases of Central Asia, and with the exception of several periods over the past two thousand years have ruled themselves autonomously along the trade routes of the old Silk Road. In 1755, the Qing Dynasty led by a Manchu government invaded parts of the region. They made it a tenuously controlled provincial level territory in 1884, establishing military outposts in key urban areas. At the founding of the People's Republic of China in 1949, the population of Han-identified inhabitants of the region was around 6 percent, with Uyghurs comprising roughly 80 percent of the population—and nearly all of the population in their ancestral homelands in the southern part of the region.

Prior to 1949, it was unclear whether the region would become an East Turkestan republic within the Soviet Union or whether the imperial boundaries of the Qing Dynasty would turn Uyghur and Kazakh lands into an internal colony of the People's Republic. However, in 1949, Stalin and Chinese Communist Party leaders agreed that China should "occupy" the region. In the 1950s, the Chinese state moved several million former soldiers into the northern part of the region to work as farmers

14   on military colonies. These settlers, members of the Xinjiang
Production and Construction Corps, were pulled into the bor-
derlands through a combination of economic incentives and
ideological persuasion. In addition to the Han settlers, nearly a
million Chinese-speaking Muslims called Hui, the group Vera
was from, have also moved into the region. Today, Uyghurs com-
prise less than 50 percent of the total population, and the Han
now make up more than 40 percent. The region has become the
source of around 20 percent of China's oil and natural gas. It has
an even higher percentage of China's coal reserves, and produces
around a quarter of the world's cotton and tomatoes.

During the early decades of the People's Republic, the Han
settlers largely remained isolated from Uyghurs. Because of the
lack of roads and the immense mountain range that separated
the Han-occupied lands to the north and Uyghur lands to the
south, the vast majority of Uyghurs and Han settlers did not
encounter each other in their daily activities. While the Chinese Communist Party did transform the governance structure
of the region, in the southern areas Uyghurs maintained leadership positions. The few Han who were stationed in the south
adapted to the cultural traditions of the Uyghur world, even as
Uyghur religious leaders were banished as part of the purges of
the Cultural Revolution.

The relative autonomy the Uyghurs enjoyed in the south of
the region began to change in the 1990s as China shifted toward
an export-driven market economy. As China became the "factory of the world," oil, natural gas, and eventually cotton and
tomatoes became the pillars of the Xinjiang economy. The search
for these commodities drew millions of Han settlers into the
Uyghur-majority areas of the region, first to build the resource

extraction infrastructure and then supporting industries and
service sectors. Over the past three decades, Xinjiang has come
to serve as a classic peripheral colony—catering to the needs
of the metropoles in Shanghai and Shenzhen. As in other settler colonial projects, the native peoples were largely excluded
from the most lucrative aspects of the new economy. When the
settler economy precipitated a rise in the cost of living, the
expanding urban and resource sectors placed increasing pressure on Uyghur households. While some became tenant farmers
in the industrial-scale cotton farms, many were pushed into
low-paid migrant work in construction and other sectors.

The shifting economy and political dynamics brought
about by the settler migration of the 1990s also precipitated a
rise in cycles of protest and violence. For instance, in the township of Barin, near the city of Kashgar, Uyghur farmers armed
with hunting rifles and farming tools mounted what is frequently referred to as an "uprising" against the implementation
of family planning policies and the preferential treatment of
Han settlers who were offered jobs and irrigation rights. While
some of the framing of the Uyghur occupation of township government buildings in the incident did center around greater
Uyghur self-determination—what the state would describe
first as ethnic separatism, and later terrorism—what stood out
to the Uyghur intellectual Abduweli Ayup, who was living in the
region at the time, was the way the protests were "crushed by
the Chinese military." In a memoir he recalls how "the government followed up with mass arrests." He remembers the way

eyewitness accounts circulated in my village describing
how protesters were loaded like bricks in trucks and

16   hauled away. The police not only took custody of the living
        but also the bodies of the dead. At the time, all schools
        were forced to close and everyone was forced to partici-
        pate in political indoctrination sessions. It is still fresh
        in my memory, at that time when homes were searched,
        religious books were burnt, and people were randomly
        arrested. There were also quiet murmurings among our-
        selves, knowing that the government was accusing us, the
        victims of the state's policies, of being "troublemakers."

The strict enforcement of settler preferential treatment in
the Uyghur majority areas bred significant resentment. Widespread job discrimination, land seizures, and increased government control of religious practice sparked a series of protests
and violent crackdowns throughout the 1990s and early 2000s.
This rose to a head in 2009, when a Uyghur student protest in
response to the lynching of Uyghur workers by Han workers
sparked live gunfire from armed police. In response, Uyghurs
rioted in the streets of Ürümchi, killing over 130 Han civilians
and injuring many more. Over the months that followed, the
local authorities introduced a militarized "hard-strike" campaign across the region. This led to the disappearance of several
thousand Uyghurs—and more resentment around police brutality and state control.

As scholars Sean Roberts and Gardner Bovingdon have
shown, over the past three decades increased forms of control and ethnic discrimination have been the primary causes
of increased Uyghur protest and violence directed at state
actors. As the discourse of Muslim terrorism entered China in

the 2000s, many such incidents were described by state media as "terrorism." However, it is important to note in many cases the majority of the people killed or hurt in these protests-turned-incidents were Uyghur perpetrators themselves. The "terrorists" were typically unarmed or had improvised weapons and were killed or injured by the automatic weapons of the police.

Eventually, however, some violent incidents did begin to resemble what might be internationally regarded as terrorism. In late 2013 and early 2014, there was a rise of violent attacks carried out by Uyghur civilians that directly targeted Han civilians. Suicide attacks in urban centers such as Beijing, Kunming, and Ürümchi stand out in this regard. These attacks, which utilized knives, vehicles, and explosive devices, are distinctive relative to prior incidents, which were often spontaneous and targeted the police and government authorities rather than civilians. For the first time, Uyghur assailants appeared to be planning coordinated attacks that indiscriminately targeted non-Muslims. Even more troubling, they appeared to be linked not to local political and economic grievances, but instead to resemble the tactics of criminals in Europe and North America who acted on behalf of the emergent Islamic State.

Around this time, Kazakhs and Uyghurs began to participate in social media for the first time. They also became more interested in contemporary Muslim culture and faith traditions from across the Muslim world—such as those inspired by the Tablighi Jamaat, a nonpolitical Sunni piety tradition that has hundreds of thousands of members around the world. The rise of planned attacks and increasing adherence to halal standards

18   among Uyghurs in general, such as abstaining from alcohol,
      alarmed Han settlers in Xinjiang, who feared a largely abstract,
      threatening stereotype of Islamic danger.

      In addition, during this period, a population of close to ten
      thousand Uyghurs fled to Turkey via China's porous border
      with Myanmar. With the alleged support of the Turkish gov-
      ernment, over a thousand of them eventually went on to Syria
      to fight both ISIS and the Assad regime. As a proportion of the
      Uyghur population as a whole, this group of foreign fighters was
      smaller than the number of UK Muslims who also fought in the
      Syrian Civil War. But in China, the mere presence of Uyghurs in
      Syria confirmed what authorities viewed as an existential threat
      to Chinese sovereignty. In echoes of Cultural Revolution—
      era rhetoric that depicted counterrevolutionaries as vermin,
      state media began to represent Uyghurs and Kazakhs who were
      deemed extremists as venomous snakes and disease-carrying
      insects who needed to be exterminated.

      In response to the attacks carried out by several dozen
      individuals and supported by hundreds more, the rise in pious
      Islamic practice, and the exodus of Uyghur refugees to Turkey,
      Chinese state authorities declared the "People's War on Terror."
      However, unlike domestic counter-terrorism campaigns in
      Europe and North America, the "People's War" precipitated an
      extrajudicial mass internment program in defense of the set-
      tler society in the Uyghur ancestral lands. Rather than targeting
      a small number of criminals, the campaign targeted the entire
      Muslim population of 15 million in Xinjiang. It precipitated a
      criminalization of Islamic practice and a number of Uyghur and
      Kazakh cultural traditions. Initially only religious leaders were
      sent to camps, but by 2017 the war on terror became a program

of preventing Uyghurs from being Muslim and, to a certain
extent, from being Uyghur or Kazakh.

In the space of half a decade, the state built a system of check-points first between counties and then within urban jurisdictions. They established a passcard system that restricted the movement of Uyghurs within the region and confiscated passports from the few Uyghurs and Kazakhs who had obtained them. They sent as many as 1.1 million state workers into Uyghur and Kazakh rural communities to conduct assessments of the "untrustworthy" Muslims. They hired over ninety thousand additional assistant police who were tasked with scanning Muslim phones and IDs, producing a density in policing that rivaled East Germany before the fall of the Berlin Wall. They also began building a network of highly securitized internment camps, which at the height of detentions would hold between 10 to 20 percent of the adult population—the proportion of the population that regional authorities deemed to have developed the "tumors" of religious extremism. At the same time, the state's Civil Affairs Ministry began to enforce a "zero illegal births" policy that, along with endemic family separation caused by detentions, precipitated a drop in birth rates of 50 to 80 percent.

In April 2018, in Kashgar city, where there were checkpoints every two hundred meters, I encountered police assistants who asked me to show them my ID. They scanned my passport and ran it through an image recognition system looking for matches with individuals on the watch list. While they detained me at one checkpoint I observed the way they asked every passing Uyghur for their smartphones, so they could inspect them using an app made by either the digital forensics companies

20 Meiya Pico or FiberHome. Both companies were working in the region to turn smartphones into tracking devices. I imagined being questioned about the hundreds of Uyghurs I had interviewed since 2011.

From their relatives and friends I learned that nearly three dozen of the people I knew had disappeared into the camp system, but most of my closest Uyghur and Kazakh friends were still outside the camps. I thought about the images of checkpoints, camera systems, signs, and technical equipment on SD cards that the police could easily find in an inner pocket of my bag with a simple metal detector. The pages and pages of notes on disappearances and surveillance equipment they might find hidden in a password-protected drive on my laptop. How they would force me to give them my email passwords. I imagined being shackled and thrown into a crowded concrete cell, being forced to sign a confession that said I was secretly working for a US intelligence agency—something I would later be accused of in a public statement by a Xinjiang government spokesperson.

State authorities had outsourced authority to private technology companies and police contractors in an attempt to transform the native populations of the region. Private industrialists and Han settlers, who had benefited from the natural resource economy, were called into action to implement a surveillance industry at the cutting edge of contemporary technological systems. This digital enclosure moved from face-scan checkpoints and smartphone scanners to smart camps and factories.

State authorities and state affiliated media refer to this massive internment campaign as Transformation through Education. In documents submitted to the UN, Chinese state

authorities describe this system as a "vocational training program" for Xinjiang citizens whose terrorism or religious
extremism violations did not rise to the level of criminality,
who had violated counter-terrorism guidelines unintentionally,
or who had previously served a prison sentence for terrorism-
and extremism-related crimes. Many of these violations had to
do with online activity and mosque attendance. For instance, a
manual used by state workers tasked with assessing the Uyghur
and Kazakh populations described simply using a VPN—as
Vera had—or visiting foreign websites as equivalent to planning to carry out terrorist acts. An internal police report noted
that visiting a mosque "more than two hundred times" would
result in a Muslim being sent "for education" in the camps. In
the mosque featured in the report, this threat—along with a
face-scan checkpoint at the entrance of the mosque—had precipitated a 96 percent drop in attendance in a single year.

As a result of these policies, Chinese authorities have
placed as many as 1.5 million Uyghurs, Kazakhs, and Hui into
a system of medium- to maximum-security "reeducation"
camps since 2017—making it the largest internment of a religious minority since World War II. This archipelago of over
three hundred camps and other newly built or expanded extra-
judicial detention facilities has been documented through government bid contracts, satellite imagery, researcher visits, and
interviews with former detainees and former camp workers. In
addition, state documents and interviews with former workers
show that the Chinese state has utilized a dispersed network
of corporate-incentivized forced labor programs and unprecedented surveillance technologies to control, track, monitor, and

22 extract data and labor from hundreds of thousands of Muslims who remain outside the camp.

Based on my interviews and media reports, some detainees have also been transferred to prisons. According to the Xinjiang state prosecutor's office, between 2017 and 2020, over 533,000 people were formally prosecuted in Xinjiang, a rate six times higher than the national average for that period. Since the conviction rates in Chinese courts are higher than 99 percent, it is safe to assume that nearly all criminal prosecutions resulted in formal sentences. Some former detainees, particularly the elderly and infirm, have been placed under forms of community monitoring and house arrest. Hundreds of thousands more have been placed in forms of coerced and controlled labor in factories associated with the camps. In a general sense, state authorities and private manufactures now control significant aspects of everyday Muslim life. The technologies involved in this system of control have given rise to a profit-making industry entangled with the state, making the repression of minority citizens profitable for national and local governments. While similarly comprehensive totalitarian systems have targeted ethnic minorities in the previous century, this is the first effort of such scale to emerge in the era of digital surveillance. This is what makes it a new phenomenon in the history of colonialism and camp systems.

The system is premised on a rhetoric of a war on Muslim "terrorism" that the Chinese state has imported from the US and its allies post–September 11, 2001. As recently as 2017, Xinjiang authorities hosted British counter-terrorism experts as part of a diplomatic exchange called "Countering the root causes of violent extremism undermining growth and stability

in China's Xinjiang Region by sharing UK best practice." In the
Chinese context, countering violent extremism—something
that British experts refer to simply as *Prevent*—is premised on
detaining hundreds of thousands of Muslims deemed "untrustworthy" in camps and prisons, and placing still other Muslim
adults in jobs far from their homes. As many as five hundred
thousand children have been placed in residential boarding
schools. The logics of counter-terrorism have been used to
grossly supersede concerns with human and civil rights, creating an immense high-tech penal colony.

As in other contexts, the costs of wars on terror have been
largely borne by Muslims themselves. The detainability of
"pre-criminals," such as Muslim citizens suspected of terrorism links, is produced by the state through legal mechanisms that place them outside the civil protections granted
to non-Muslims. Muslims around the world have been put on
watch lists. This slotting of subordinated populations into the
category of the "terrorist" helps to justify state power while
simultaneously producing data-intensive surveillance industries. This rhetoric has produced a category of legal inde-
terminacy that means Muslims like Vera can be treated with
impunity. The difference in China is the immense scale of the
watchlists and camps, and the way they are shaped by advanced
technologies.

This book draws on more than twenty-four months of ethnographic research in Xinjiang, Kazakhstan, and Seattle between
2011 and 2020. It examines thousands of verified government
texts, tech industry documents, and internal Chinese police
reports that have been leaked by government officials and

24   others in the technology industry. But its central propulsion is dozens of long interviews with Kazakh, Uyghur, and Hui former detainees, camp workers, and system technicians. Some of these interviewees were Kazakhs who were able to use family connections and a kind of "birthright" immigration program to flee across the border to Kazakhstan. Even fewer were able to board planes to the US and Europe by convincing authorities that they would not speak out. Some of them—Vera, Baimurat, Qelbinur, Erbaqyt, and Gulzira—asked me to use their real names. The others asked that I rename them in order to protect their family members back home in China. This book is their story.

As they told me about the technological enclosure of their homeland, I saw the way technologies of reeducation made Muslims detainable. The surveillance system itself produced assumptions of guilt, of pre-criminality. As the system manufactured these claims, many Muslims were made to hide their moral objections by wearing masks of loyalty to the state program. Those who lacked these masks were dehumanized under the lights and cameras of the camps. They were transformed by plastic stools, electric batons, and automated cruelty. They were trained to sit still, to cower when appropriate, to accept beatings silently, to sing loudly, to always smile, and to say, "Yes!" to every command. They were conditioned not to register the smell of excrement, sweat, and fear that came with the open buckets used as toilets, the crush of unwashed bodies in cramped space, and their terror of the guards. They stopped noticing the glare of bright lights in the middle of the night. They stopped feeling their constant hunger. They stopped thinking about the distant future or the past.

Many, especially the hundreds of thousands of rural Uyghurs who have no one to speak for them, are still there. But some have been released back into the digital enclosure as unfree workers under the gaze of the "smart" factories.

The former detainees told me that they do not blame the technicians and camp workers who feed and maintain the machine of indifference under conditions of coercion. They blame the bosses who mandate the system, the ones who laugh at their misery. And they hold the designers and engineers who created the technologies responsible. As I listened to them, I came to the unsettling conclusion that the dehumanization they experienced was created at least in part in computer labs from Seattle to Beijing.

Pre-crime

Vera Zhou didn't think the war on terror had anything to do with her. She considered herself a non-religious fashionista who favored chunky earrings and dressing in black. She had gone to high school near Portland, Oregon, and was on her way to becoming an urban planner at a top-ranked university in the United States. After she graduated, she had planned to reunite with her boyfriend and have a career in China, where she thought of the economy as booming under the leadership of Xi Jinping. Since her father and boyfriend were Han, she assumed that she would be protected, even though her ID said she was a Muslim. She had no idea that a new internet security law had been implemented in her hometown and across Xinjiang at the beginning of 2017, and that this was how extremist "pre-criminals," as state authorities referred to them, were being identified for detention. She did not know that a newly appointed party secretary of the region had given a command to "round up everyone who should be rounded up" as part of the Xi Jinping–approved "People's War."

Now, in the back of the van, she felt herself losing control in a wave of fear. She screamed, tears streaming down her face, "Why are you doing this? Doesn't our country protect the innocent?" It seemed to her like it was a cruel joke, like she had been given a role in a horror movie, and that if she just said the right things they might snap out of it and realize it was all a mistake.

Eventually the commanding officer told her, "It would be better for you if you shut up." Then she began to sob silently, looking out the window, looking for the lights of her boyfriend's car, watching the steppe rush by in the early morning light. After several minutes, the window she was looking out of began to fog over. When none of the other police officers were looking, the young police contractor leaned over and silently cleared the condensation off the window with a swipe of his hand. Vera said, "I'll never forget that moment. Although he could not show any sympathy, through his gesture he showed me that at least some of the people who are responsible for this are still human."

This short book tells the story of this global rise in complex digital enclosures and automated monitoring systems at the cutting edge of "smart" social control by examining a limited case of their use in China. What is happening in Northwest China is connected to camps at the southern border of the United States, digital control in Kashmir, and checkpoints in the West Bank, but its scale and cruelty takes it beyond those other sites of exceptional power over marginalized populations. In China these systems of control become "reeducation technologies" that produce new kinds of laborers, people like Vera who are held both in material and virtual detention. Even if people are not formally detained, the use of facial recognition technologies

28   and datasets of flagged behaviors permits legal policing regimes
      to convert populations of the undetained into data. This, in
      turn, forces those populations to adapt to controlled environ-
      ments, making them an unfree and dependent workforce.

          Yet, despite the banal everydayness of these technological
      and material systems, this book also considers how humans
      still have the capacity to refuse, to denarrativize their exis-
      tence, opening up space for thinking with, and acting against,
      incomprehensible violence. These moments of refusing to let
      go of humanity—whether caring for other humans by clearing
      the glass, or shedding a tear—punctures the façade of this inhu-
      mane system. It is these actions that make the machine of reed-
      ucation stutter. They are what keep people living despite the
      banality of unfreedom. As Primo Levi put it in his reflections on
      his time in Auschwitz, besides being in good health, knowing
      the language of the police, and having international allies, sur-
      viving camp systems is often based primarily on "sheer luck."
      But this luck is shaped in turn by a willful stubbornness and
      the refusal to deny their own humanity. As I have written this
      book, I have thought often about the continuities and rup-
      tures between this camp system and the ones that came before.
      From the perspective of those who survive with their humanity
      intact, much remains true to Levi's experience. Vera, and many
      of the other figures who narrate the processes of the camp
      system in this book, found that by persisting, by refusing to give
      up, chance occasionally opened up to sympathy and gaps in the
      midst of unprecedented high tech surveillance.

      For the next couple of months, Vera was held with eleven other
      Muslim minority women in a second-floor cell in a former

police station on the outskirts of Kuitun. Like Vera, others in the
room were also guilty of cyber "pre-crimes." A Kazakh woman
had installed WhatsApp on her phone in order to contact business partners in Kazakhstan. A Uyghur woman who sold smartphones at a bazaar had allowed multiple customers to register
their SIM cards using her ID card.

The guards told her that she was not in jail, but rather at
a "centralized controlled education training center." The term
they used for centralized (*jizhong*) can also mean "concentrated,"
a connection that was not lost on Vera. She told me, "I learned
almost right away that it was a kind of concentration camp. The
guards knew we were not guilty of anything. Everyone in my cell
was innocent of any real crime. They just took us because the
leaders said to detain the Muslims." During her first days in the
camp, she whispered the stories she had read about the Holo-
caust back in her high school in Portland to her fellow detainees.
She told them, "What is happening to us is just like what happened to Anne Frank."

When she first arrived, a camera system had not yet been
installed in the cell. It felt to Vera like the authorities were
still in the process of converting the old police station into the
camp—seven months after the mass detentions began. "They
didn't even have enough bowls for everyone to eat out of, so we
had to share."

The lack of preparedness also had its advantages. Whenever the guards were out of earshot, the detainees could chat
with each other. Vera learned that a young Kazakh woman in
the cell spoke perfect Mandarin and had also studied abroad
in the Pacific Northwest at a university in Vancouver. Over the
first few days, they talked about everything. "We talked about

30   food, her job experience as a doctor, books, movies, restaurants, about whether or not we had been to the Space Needle. It was as if we were not in the camp. It was as though the camp was just a bad dream."

The others in the cell listened in on their conversations as best they could, though most of the elderly Uyghur and Kazakh women did not really understand Mandarin since their native languages were so different from Chinese. Their lack of understanding was made painfully obvious when the guards attempted to make them memorize ten rules that were posted on the wall of the cell. Vera recalled how they stumbled over phrases like, "Only speak the language of the country; Love the motherland; Oppose harm to the motherland; There is no religion in this room; Do not damage the TV or anything on the walls; No fighting; No one is allowed to speak secretly; No one is allowed to speak to students in other cells; Sit on your stools."

At night, staring up at the extraordinarily bright lights, which were never turned off, it was hard to forget what was happening. Vera still remembers the sound of muffled crying, a sound that moved through the crowded cell like a contagion. "It took me about a month to get used to having the lights on."

Around the time that she was just beginning to sleep with less difficulty, they were moved into a new cell that had a state-of-the-art camera and audio recording system that monitored their movements. The guards' voices would boom out of a speaker mounted on the wall if they covered their eyes with a hand or blanket to block out the bright light. They also received warnings if they tried to sit on their beds except during prescribed sleep time or spoke anything other than Mandarin.

During the day, they were only permitted to stand or sit on plastic stools while they watched "reeducation" TV programs on a monitor mounted on the wall.

Around January 2018, after a new wing of the camp was completed, there was a dramatic increase in new detainees. Although she was not able to see into each room, Vera estimated that by that point at least six hundred people were detained in the camp—more than 10 percent of the total adult population of Kazakhs and Uyghurs in Kuitun. She imagined that by that time nearly all Uyghur families and most Kazakh families in town were missing a parent. "They brought so many Uyghur and Kazakh people at that time," Vera remembered. "Three or four people every night. Whole families were brought in together. They had to sleep on the concrete floor." One of the women they brought in was a young mother. In a small gesture of sympathy the guards had allowed her to keep a picture of her baby boy, who she was still breastfeeding. "At night she kept looking at her son's picture and crying. Since the guards could see this on the camera, they yelled at her over the speaker, 'If you look at your son's picture and cry again, we will take it away.'"

The dehumanizing discipline of the camp repelled detainees, pushing them to fear each other. In a grotesque parody of the Chinese education system, during a private meeting with her cell's "life teacher"—a Civil Affairs Ministry employee who took on the role of "class advisor," as is common in the Chinese education system—Vera was secretly assigned the job of a "class monitor." "She asked me to spy on other people," Vera recalled. "I tried really hard not to say anything bad about others in my cell, but every week our 'life teacher' would ask me about others in the cell. If someone did not do well the previous week with following the rules or reciting Chinese, I would just say this or that person was sick."

The life teacher asked each detainee to write a self-confession, or "thought report," every week. "These were some of the scariest moments of life in the camp," Vera recalled. She knew that every week she had to show "progress" or else she would never be allowed to leave, but if she admitted to too many thought crimes it could result in her being given a prison sentence. "Once per month the life teacher would arrange for us to talk to the warden for one hour. You had to tell him what you think you did wrong. He would ask, 'Why did you do this?' I would say, 'I know I used a VPN and that this did not protect the security of our country.' He would say, 'Think deeply why you did this, tell me why from the deepest part of your heart. Why would we put you in the camp instead of others? Tell us the reason. Do you love our country?' It was so intense. Even now it makes me shake thinking about it."

Back in the cell, Vera helped her Uyghur and Kazakh cellmates write their "thought reports." She wrote about their "pre-crimes" in different ways each time. But they didn't understand the Chinese characters and did not know what to say to the life teacher, so they never even got their chance in front of the warden.

As the months wore on, Vera became more and more despondent. She was demoted from her role as class monitor because she refused to report a detainee who was passing notes to others. The male guards marched the Uyghur note-writer away. They never saw her again. The mindless recitation of rules, the first grade–level Chinese lessons that played on the TV monitor while they sat on their plastic stools, and the party-state anthems they were forced to sing before their meals became an endless looping soundtrack of the camp. "The most terrifying thing about being there was not knowing if you would ever be released," Vera said.

Back in the United States, Vera's mother, Caiyun Ma, was becoming more and more desperate. Understanding the authority of health care and educational institutions as a counter to the authority of the police, she asked me to write a letter on university letterhead attesting that Vera was an outstanding student and was missing her classes in Seattle. She also obtained a document from Vera's doctor in Oregon describing how fragile Vera's health was following a bout with cancer the year before. After getting the documents translated and certified with official stamps, she sent them to her ex-husband, Vera's father, back in Kuitun. Although he was deeply fearful, Vera's father delivered the letters to the camp.

Several months into her detention, police officers marched Vera out of the facility with bayoneted automatic weapons pointed at her back. They shackled her hands behind her back and sat her down in a cold minibus. After what seemed like hours, they removed the hood and led her into a hospital where a doctor gave her a cursory exam. Then the guards took her back to the camp. Initially it appeared that our attempt to introduce the fear of "abnormal death" and to imply the potential of a violation of "strict secrecy," terms used by Chinese state authorities to describe prohibitions on detainee death and leaking classified secrets about the extralegal conditions of the camp, had failed.

34   Then around a month later, without warning, Vera and several other detainees were released on the provision that they
report to local social stability workers on a regular basis and not
try to leave their home neighborhoods. When she got out of the
minibus at the government office in her neighborhood, her probation officer said, "'Oh, we finally got you out.' I thought, 'How
could she say something like this? She was one of the people
who put me in that place and now she was pretending she was
my friend.'"

Every Monday, her probation officer required that Vera go to
a neighborhood flag-raising ceremony and participate by loudly
singing the Chinese national anthem and making statements
pledging her loyalty to the Chinese government. By this time,
due to widely circulated reports of detention for cyber-crimes
in the small town, it was known that online behavior could be
detected by the newly installed automated internet surveillance systems. Like everyone else, Vera recalibrated her online
behavior. Whenever the social stability worker assigned to her
shared something on social media, Vera was always the first
person to support her by liking it and posting it on her own
account. Like everyone else she knew, she started to "spread
positive energy" by actively promoting state ideology.

After she was back in her neighborhood, she felt that she
had changed. She thought often about the hundreds of detainees
she had seen in the camp. She feared that many of them would
never be allowed out since they didn't know Chinese and had
been practicing Muslims their whole lives. She said her time in
the camp also made her question her own sanity. "Sometimes I
thought maybe I don't love my country enough. Maybe I only
thought about myself. Maybe I wasn't careful enough. I think we

all started to think about this to a certain degree. Maybe I didn't
help the Party and the country. I just helped my family. I didn't
take my responsibility."

But she also knew that what had happened to her was not
her fault. It was the result of Islamophobia being institution-
alized and focused on her. Although she could pass as Han, she
now always thought, "What if . . . ?" And she knew with absolute certainty that an immeasurable cruelty was being done to
Uyghurs and Kazakhs because of their ethno-racial, linguistic,
and religious differences. By comparison, Hui people like her
had it easy.

She noticed that her father was also more careful. Before,
he would argue with the local social stability officers. Now he
always greeted them effusively. During their visits to monitor
her progress "he always agreed with them," she remembered.
"He told them 'studying was good for me.'"

Like all 25 million permanent residents of Xinjiang, before
Vera was taken to the camp she had been subject to a biometric
data collection process called "physicals for all." The police had
scanned Vera's face and irises, recorded her voice signature, and
collected her blood, fingerprints, and DNA—adding this precise high-fidelity data to an immense dataset that was being
used to map the behavior of the population of the region. They
had also taken her phone away to have it and her social media
accounts scanned for Islamic imagery, connections to for-
eigners, and other signs of "extremism." Eventually they gave it
back, without any of the US-made apps like Instagram, which
she had used before.

For a short period of time, she began to find ways around
the many checkpoints. Since she could pass as Han and spoke

36   standard Mandarin, she would simply tell the security workers that she forgot her ID and would write down a fake number. Or sometimes she would go through the exit of the checkpoint, "the green lane," just like a Han person and ignore the police. One time, though, when going to see a movie with a friend, she forgot to pretend that she was Han. At a checkpoint at the theater she put her ID on the scanner and looked into the camera. Immediately an alarm sounded and the mall police contractors pulled her to the side. As her friend disappeared into the crowd, Vera worked her phone frantically to delete her social media account and erase the contacts of people who might be detained because of their association with her. "I realized then that it really wasn't safe to have friends. I just started to stay at home all the time."

Eventually, like many former detainees, Vera was forced to work as an unpaid laborer. The local state police commander in her neighborhood learned that she had spent time in the United States as a college student. So he asked Vera's probation officer to assign her to tutor his children in English. "I thought about asking him to pay me," Vera remembers. "But my dad said I need to do it for free. He also sent food with me for them, to show how eager he was to please them." The commander never brought up any form of payment.

Vera was isolated and individuated as an unfree worker. She became a nanny, caring for the police officer's children while he was working in the reeducation system.

In October 2019, Vera's probation officer told her that she was happy with Vera's progress and she would be allowed to continue her education back in Seattle. She was made to sign vows not to talk about what she had experienced. The officer

said, "Your father has a good job and will soon reach retirement
age. Remember this."

Now back in the United States, Vera is beginning to resume her studies at the University of Washington in the midst of a pandemic. In the two years that she has been gone, her friends, most of whom were also international students from China, have graduated and moved on. There is a blank spot in her young life. She tells herself over and over that what happened to her was not her fault: "There was no reason for this. It was random. There was no reason."

Phone Disaster

Qeyser saw a phone for the first time in 2005, when he was fifteen years old. In his village, mobile phones arrived before landlines, which is common in the developing world. "The first phone I ever saw was the flip phone of the vice-secretary of our village's work brigade unit," Qeyser recalled. "It was pretty simple, but looked really complicated to me. It had all these numbers and letters. I thought, 'How could he call and write at the same time?'" This moment was seared into Qeyser's memory. It signified that the future was coming to Uyghur villages. He and the other children and teenagers followed the Communist Party leader from place to place as he searched for a signal. "He would speak in a loud voice to whoever was on the other end of the phone, making a big show of it. It was like magic. He turned on the speaker function and then all of us started talking loudly to the person who was far away at the other end."

By 2007, landlines were built into the village. People who could afford the service began to install "house phones" and charge the neighbors to use them. "Many people used their house phone to make money," Qeyser remembered. "They would charge people to use them. One minute, ten cents; five minutes, fifty cents. That was a very interesting time. If you went to a friend's house and they had a phone, we would hold the phone up to our ear and listen to the sound. We would pretend to call and speak like we were important businesspeople. It was a joyful thing."

By 2008, the signal from cell towers for basic service reached the village and many people, including Qeyser's family, bought a simple Nokia. But at that time cell phones were just for communication, not accessing the internet. "No one knew about texting. Most people didn't know how to send or receive messages or images until 2010 when 3G arrived," he recalled.

It wasn't until Qeyser was in college in the city of Ürümchi that he first learned about social media in a smoke-filled internet cafe. The platform QQ, which he accessed on a monitor in rows of boxy desktop computers, gave him a chance to develop an online persona. QQ, which mimicked some of the features of MySpace and Facebook, was the first platform that allowed them to experiment with social networking. "Everyone wanted to make a homepage that represented who they were to the world," Qeyser recalled. "We chose lots of pictures of beautiful people and places to represent our hopes and dreams." In the city, Uyghur young people spent a lot of time in these all-night cafes playing computer games and lurking in QQ chatrooms. But computers were still not mainstream. Instead, the internet was something that a minority of migrants and urbanites were beginning to explore. Because software to type in Uyghur-language Arabic script was just being developed and few Uyghurs had been trained in how to type using

40   keyboards, the internet and the world of knowledge it offered
      them remained on the horizon. Or it was filtered through Chi-
      nese language text.

          In late spring 2009, grainy images, videos, and text mes-
      sages circulated on QQ and another Facebook-inspired Chi-
      nese app called Renren of a lynching of Uyghur workers. The
      attacks on the workers, who had been transferred to a factory in
      Eastern China as part of a government labor transfer program,
      produced a short-lived viral sensation on the nascent Uyghur
      internet. Uyghurs poured into the internet cafes to see the pic-
      tures and speak heatedly about the lack of response from the
      government. Students organized a march, waving Chinese flags
      and demanding that the authorities arrest the Han workers
      who had killed several Uyghurs and beaten dozens more in the
      graphic videos. Eventually, the police opened fire on the protes-
      tors, which precipitated a citywide riot. Over two days, Uyghur
      migrants beat over 130 Han people to death. The following
      day, as the armed police and military descended on the city,
      Han migrants beat dozens of Uyghurs to death as police stood
      by watching the hand-to-hand combat with kitchen cleavers,
      bricks pulled up from the sidewalks, and sharpened sticks. At
      night, witnesses heard the sound of automatic gunfire from the
      police echoing through the streets in Uyghur-majority areas.

          In the weeks that followed, the police took away thousands
      of Uyghurs accused of participating in the rioting. The local
      authorities also turned off the internet across the entire region.
      For more than nine months, communications in the region were
      tightly restricted, before the internet returned in mid-2010.
      And now, new 3G networks allowed millions of Uyghurs in vil-
      lages across the region to get online. The intuitive design of

cheap Chinese-made smartphones allowed farmers with little
training in technology to begin to explore and communicate.

This process of becoming digital persons was dramatically
accelerated by a new smartphone-specific app called WeChat,
developed by Tencent. This app, which combines some of the
features of WhatsApp and Twitter, has since become one of the
world's most widely used social media platforms, with around
1.2 billion users. Since Facebook and Twitter and all other
non-Chinese apps had been blocked across the entire country
in 2009, Uyghur internet users focused their online communication on WeChat. And because they could send recorded voice
memos in Uyghur on the app, the problems with Uyghur language keyboards and lack of training in typing were no longer an
issue. In the space of only a couple of years, millions of Uyghurs
purchased smartphones and were using the app on a daily basis
to build networks of friends. They also discovered that using
the voice memo function allowed them to have Uyghur conversations at least partially outside of the censorship capacities of
Chinese state authorities.

Uyghurs, Kazakhs, and Hui people began to use WeChat
forums to discuss religious and cultural knowledge, political
events, and economic opportunities outside their local communities. Over the course of only a few years, online Islamic teachers
based in the region and elsewhere in the Islamic world, in places
like Turkey and Uzbekistan, became influential throughout
Uyghur WeChat. Their messages focused primarily on Islamic
piety. They described what types of practices were halal, and how
people should dress and pray. According to scholars Rachel Harris
and Aziz Isa, the vast majority of those who began to study Islam
by smartphone were simply interested in instruction on what it

42   might mean to be a contemporary Muslim, something they felt
was lacking in government-censored state-run mosques.

Young Uyghur migrants around Qeyser's age used WeChat
to find economic opportunities, to follow the news of the Gezi
Park protests in Istanbul, and to join Islamic piety movements.
Although many of these young men struggled to find secure
employment in the city, WeChat provided them with a community network in which to find a social role. Since the oral speech
function of the app did not require a high level of computer lit-
eracy and data plans were relatively cheap, smartphone usage
began to shape the basic fabric of their daily lives. Initially, most
of them did not realize that the sporadic violent attacks and protests that were happening across the region and country could
be construed through an Islamophobic lens as an outgrowth of
religious piety. Many young Uyghurs I spoke with at the time
did not realize that their relative freedom online was primarily
a product of the inability of state authorities and the Chinese
tech industry to assess Uyghur oral and written speech, not an
invitation to greater self-determination.

The People's War on Terror
Chinese authorities, and many non-Muslim citizens, took a
different view of this digital phenomenon. They regarded the
changing Islamic appearance and practice of Uyghurs, such as
young men growing beards and praying five times per day, as
signs of what they described as the "extremification" of the
Uyghur population. State authorities began to link violent
incidents—such as a suicide attack in the city of Kunming in
Southwest China deemed "China's 9/11", to what government
officials told me was a process of "Talibanization." Likewise,

media coverage of the rise of the Islamic State filled local officials with the feeling of imminent threat. In response to this,
Chinese authorities declared what they called a "People's War
on Terror." They began to use techniques of counterinsurgency,
a mode of military engagement that stresses mass intelligence
gathering, to assess the Uyghur, Kazakh, and Hui populations,
which they believed were full of terrorists-in-hiding.

Chinese state authorities began to circulate a list of seventy-
five official signs of Islamic extremism. Things like possession
of digital files with religious content, using a VPN, or installing
WhatsApp—an encrypted social media platform that was
acquired by Facebook in 2014—were categorized as "pre-crimes"
that could lead to detention. Because WhatsApp was the most
widely used app in Kazakhstan and Turkey, authorities assumed
that Uyghurs using the app were attempting to engage with the
Muslim world, and doing so outside of the censorship and surveillance systems of the Chinese internet. Initially, the state did
not have the capacity to detect the use of these technologies, so
even if they had heard that these bans were announced, many
Uyghurs and Kazakh assumed they would not be enforced.
They thought they would be like many other regulations that
were announced, but not put in place. But as the "People's War"
swung into motion, state authorities began outsourcing the
policing of cyberspace to private companies.

In widely circulated news articles, the giant retail platform Alibaba—an early investor in the leading face recognition
company Megvii , whose rise I will discuss in the final chapter
of this book—discussed its new role in countering the threat
of domestic "terrorism" through the algorithmic assessment
of calls, traffic, shopping, dating, email, chat records, videos,

44   language, and voiceprint detection. Along with the voice recognition company iFLYTEK—a key partner of the digital
forensics firms Meiya Pico and FiberHome—Alibaba noted
that their western counterparts, Amazon and Google, were
already doing their part in surveilling Muslim American citizens in the American version of counter-terrorism. They said
that it was time they played a similar active role in fighting
China's domestic war on Muslim terrorism.

The Chinese tech firms drew on an intelligence-led policing
program called the Golden Shield project that had already
been established post-9/11 by the Chinese Ministry of State
Security—China's version of the CIA. But they also took note
of Edward Snowden's revelations of the American government's
PRISM mass data analytics project that collected and assessed
data from social media both in the United States and around the
globe to build watch lists. And they began to adapt the techniques of US government contractors such as Palantir—a data
analysis company that scrapes and assesses social media data to
surveil people in real-time—to the context of Northwest China.

The Chinese tech companies also took advantage of a more
general shift in the Chinese economy toward public-private
partnerships, which were thought to be more responsive to economic and political challenges than reliance on Maoist-legacy
state-owned enterprises. They pitched their surveillance "solutions" to central and regional governments just as the People's
War on Terror swung into motion. By 2017, the Chinese state
had invested more than $2.6 trillion in private partnerships
in a wide range of infrastructure projects across the country.
According to some estimates, the Chinese security technology
industry as a whole reached close to $100 billion, with more

than 50 percent of the industry focused on domestic security
engineering projects.

In Xinjiang, the state awarded an estimated $65 bil-
lion in private contracts to build infrastructure and $160 bil-
lion more to government entities in the region—an increase
of 50 percent from 2016. This new investment made it one
of the largest receivers of state capital in the country. While
some of this increase in construction spending was centered
on non-security-related projects, significant portions of state
spending in Xinjiang centered on the building of detention
facilities and related infrastructure. State contractors also used
these funds to develop new tools in the region's surveillance
system and the Muslim "reeducation" campaign. Although the
state froze funding for some of these projects near the end of
2017, by 2018 the market, solely for security and information
technology in Xinjiang, grew to an estimated $8 billion, with
close to 1,400 private firms competing for lucrative contracts.

The widespread private contracting of public services
throughout the Chinese economy has produced a market structure in the technology sector, particularly in artificial intelligence, in which company growth is closely tied to state-driven
infrastructure projects that use technology to achieve political ends. As Martin Beraja, David Y. Yang, and Noam Yuchtman
have shown through a large-scale study of private technologies used in public policing in China, state capital investment in
data-intensive technologies is essential for the success of private computer-vision companies that focus on image and face
recognition. In their study, they demonstrate a "causal effect of
access to government data by comparing the increase in software production of firms that receive data-rich and data-scarce

public security contracts" and, in turn, the economic effects of this market structure. Ultimately, they show that the Chinese technology industry is shaped via state capital used in surveillance projects in Xinjiang in particular, and in an iterative process, by surveillance systems built elsewhere in China and on the New Silk Road. This is precisely why Chinese tech firms have been able to surpass many firms based in Europe and North America when it comes to facial recognition technologies.

Checkpoints

While these systems were being put in place, the People's War on Terror intensified. Initially the campaign relied in part on netizens who were willing to report other internet users for cyber-crimes. Local authorities offered rewards of around $300 per criminal conviction for "extremist, terrorist, or separatist" online behavior. This system of human-to-human citizen policing continued even as the state began hiring data police to conduct targeted checks.

For young Uyghurs like Qeyser, it seemed as though the "People's War" would have nothing to do with him. As he became comfortable using internet technology, the world was opening up to him as never before. Social media allowed him to develop a sophisticated urban persona and begin to influence the world around him. "I liked WeChat a lot," Qeyser recalled. "You could see the 'moments' of other people and you could chat as a group. You could send videos, or have a video call with anyone you wanted wherever they were, as long as they were also on the internet." Qeyser began to spend as much as 200 yuan ($30) per month on his LG smartphone data plan—much more than he spent on food or clothes each month. He also began to publish short videos that he made as a student on WeChat short-film forums. His most popular films went viral, reaching over eight hundred thousand viewers. Like many young Uyghurs, he came to view WeChat as an indispensable part of his social role in the Uyghur world.

While Qeyser did post some political content that could have gotten him in trouble, as a student who was watched very closely by school administrators he was too afraid to use his phone to study Islam. "I never studied the Quran on WeChat, but I know back in my village many people did this," he recalled. "Many people downloaded or shared Islamic teachings or *tabligh* on their phones too. I myself watched some videos about Uyghur politics on someone else's computer. Sometimes we would use a code to get onto YouTube. We didn't realize it was dangerous, that we were leaving a trail behind us. We just wanted to watch news about Uyghurs. Or Turkish TV shows. Or something about Uyghur history that wasn't written by the Chinese government."

In the fall of 2014, administrators in Qeyser's school in the city called a general assembly and asked all the students to turn over their phones. Since he had shared a news article on WeChat about Ilham Tohti, an Uyghur intellectual who was sentenced to life in prison because he had published policy recommendations critical of the Chinese colonization of the Uyghur homeland, Qeyser was terrified. "I just pretended to be so calm. But my heart was beating through my chest. Fortunately the teacher who checked my WeChat did not look closely. But another friend was detained because of something about the 2009 protests that someone had sent him and he had not deleted. He spent nine months in a detention center. He was beaten and tortured. They made him confess all of the crimes they said he was guilty of doing. I think he is now in a camp because of this record."

When I visited Qeyser's village in 2015, the local police asked me to unlock my phone and let them look through the contents. They flipped through my pictures and WeChat account, but did not seem to know how to work my WhatsApp or Facebook app. They didn't seem to notice that I had installed a VPN. After a couple of minutes of swiping around, they handed it back to me, convinced that I was just a researcher living in Xinjiang on a valid visa.

By 2016, the smartphone checks had become much more sophisticated. "The police would order us to get out of the bus," Qeyser told me. "The people with Xinjiang residency would line up in front of the checkpoint and have our faces scanned, and then the police would ask for our phones and plug them into a scanner."

Qeyser said that the first time this happened, he pretended that his phone didn't have any power. Perhaps because he looked like a sophisticated non-religious college student, the police officer let him go without a check. "I knew from what my friends told me that they could find something on you even if you had deleted it a long time ago." Qeyser stopped carrying his phone if he knew he would have to go through a checkpoint, and he bought a new iPhone, which he heard was much harder for the tools to scan. Just months before all Uyghurs were forced to return their passports to authorities for "safe-keeping" and mass detention of "pre-terrorists" like Vera began, I assisted Qeyser in making plans to leave China.

From the safety of North America, Qeyser learned that his brother had been sent to one of the new camps along with dozens of his relatives. "Many of my neighbors were detained because they listened to Islamic messages on their phones or shared stories that the machines deemed 'separatist.' Most of the young people were detained for either having attended religious gatherings or praying, or listening to things on their phones. My mother calls this 'the phone disaster' (*telepon balasi*)."

Digital Enclosure

The digital surveillance and enclosure system that enveloped Uyghur, Kazakh, and Hui life turned smartphones into tracking devices. The system that began with the construction of 2G cellular wireless networks in 2005 was expanded to digital overlays, which gave technology companies and state authorities the ability to watch and control movements and behavior in increasingly intimate ways. As the communications scholar Mark Andrejevic notes regarding the way systems of surveillance capitalism work in North America, digital enclosure is not exclusive to the pinging tower of a cellular network. Instead, as GPS tracking capacity is built into smartphones and automated biometric systems, the "internet of things" begins to assess patterns of movement. As a result, digital enclosures become a complex matrix that's multi-dimensional.

In Vera's hometown and Qeyser's village, China Mobile cellular networks provided service to people who used WeChat, and user activity was tracked and made available to Chinese authorities, who filtered the forum discussions and direct messages using keyword searches.

The Baidu mapping systems associated with apps on their phones tracked their movements using GPS. And this data was verified by checkpoint face scans and ID checks. In case that was not enough, data doors at the checkpoints built and serviced by the state contractor China Electronic Technology Corporation

50 made sure that the smartphone was registered to the person whose face and ID were scanned. And in high-traffic urban areas, local authorities used real-time license and face tracking camera systems built by many of China's leading camera and face recognition companies such as Sensetime, HikVision, Dahua, Yitu, and others.

These always-on, interactive surveillance systems were supplemented by forcible data collection through the plug-in automated assessments of smartphone software and content history—the type Qeyser strove to avoid. Inspections in Muslim homes used metal detectors to scan for unauthorized electronic devices. Local intelligence officers input biographical assessments that drew on banking histories, medical histories, and household registration data. Taken together, all of these various forms of information produced a digital enclosure of unprecedented scale and depth.

In a county-level town called Shawan, near the camp where Vera was held and directly across the mountains from Qeyser's village, state authorities embarked on building a "safe city" system. This project, and similar projects built throughout Xinjiang, strove to make individuals registered in the town and surrounding county searchable. The police would automatically be alerted to the movements of anyone who was on a watch list or who was from another county.

The system, at least as it was proposed, was designed to be supported by a Megvii algorithm called Face++. The algorithm was designed to assess object information such as license plates, but also to hone in on human faces, and even physical features or accessories associated with a person. Then tracking those identifiers, while gathering other social data, the Safe City system tracked human behavior information such as "communication behavior, accommodation behavior, migration behavior, financial behavior, consumer behavior, driving behavior and administrative violations." Taken together, all of this data built a specific digital portrait of each individual and their place within a social network. Over time it figured out who was associated with whom and the patterns of their typical behavior. When it came to assessing Muslims, it monitored their behavior and relationships for any sign of deviancy. The accuracy of the system depended on portrait recognition and comparison technology to do image analysis of already captured images—a system similar to Clearview AI software used by police departments in the United States. In "high-risk" areas such as mosques and bus stations, it used video analysis of real-time video—something similar to a pilot video surveillance *Prevent* project in London supported by the Japanese company NEC.

While there are some similarities between Western policing systems, which also disproportionately harm ethnoracial minorities, and those in China, there are also significant differences. In Xinjiang, the networks of cameras are much denser and supported by checkpoints and data surveillance, *and* every resident of the region has submitted their biometric data to the authorities in a comprehensive "public health" initiative. Because of the fidelity and scale of the dataset on which their algorithms are trained, the tools of the Xinjiang authorities are much more fine-tuned and invasive. Because the authorities have forced all residents of Xinjiang to register for a new state-issued ID card, they have a base library of high-definition images of each person's face, and in addition, they have collected tens of millions of images of the faces of residents who pass through the checkpoints. The Face++ and similar algo-rithms such as those from companies like YITU and Sensetime run extremely fast. As the Shawan study notes, in 0.8 seconds it can run a match of a face, and register and record notification alarms related to up to three hundred thousand targeted people. If technicians are willing to wait two-tenths of a second longer, it can do this with up to five hundred thousand people.

Much of the design and implementation of the enclosure system was represented as creating greater governance efficiency. Beginning in 2018, the Shawan administration system transi-tioned to a smartphone-driven digital model. A wide array of smartphone-based facial recognition technologies enabled this system to track individual behavior. It started with a face scan–centered state-issued photo ID system. By mid-2018, applica-tions to replace lost IDs could be done online using a smartphone camera to scan the applicant's face. In order to access social security benefits, residents of Shawan were required to use a new face-scan app. To pass through neighborhood checkpoints, residents needed to install another facial recognition app. Even rural farmer work brigades installed one to monitor villager work efficiency. All of this data was integrated into the broader Safe City system.

In many cases, it appears as though the new technology was welcomed. For example, a real estate company in Shawan adver-tised face-scan technology as a point of convenience and security. But it also seemed to create forms of inconvenience for some res-idents. For instance, the Shawan police noted the need to "debug" the system so that all legal residents could be automatically iden-tified at checkpoints, assuring that government and technology company personnel would not need to run manual checks.

Data Police

Most of the friction in the system appeared to come from the
work that was needed to operationalize and enforce the system.
Human laborers are required to fine-tune the data of all complex data-intensive systems. The scholar Lilly Irani describes
these technicians as "data janitors." The data janitors of the Safe
City system in Shawan and throughout the region were made up
of the ninety thousand police contractors who were hired across
the region at the beginning of 2017. These deputized intelligence
workers—like the young man who watched Vera in the back of
the minibus—did not have formal training like state police.
Most of them were not authorized to carry lethal weapons. In
other places in China, they would simply be referred to as "security guards" (*bao'an*), but in this context they had power over
Muslim life. Many of these low-level functionaries were hired
from Muslim populations themselves. The basic qualification for the job was having a "trustworthy" family background,
active opposition to "ethnic division and illegal religious activities," and basic working knowledge of Chinese. The spouses and
children of "Aid Xinjiang" personnel—the government "volun-
teers" from other parts of China who were tasked with reedu-
cating Muslim children and setting up factories for reeducated
forced laborers—were particularly encouraged to apply.

By mid-2017 these police contractors began a regionwide
process of checking people's devices using the AI-enabled auto-
recovery tools built by Meiya Pico, FiberHome, and other digital
forensics companies. All of this information was fed into an integrated joint operations platform that sent names of "pushes" for
people on watchlists to local police departments based on patterns of suspicious behaviors. The job of the data police was to

54   utilize these tools by performing spot checks, which centered on actively profiling passersby, stopping obviously Muslim young people like Qeyser and demanding that they show their state-issued ID and unlock their phone for automated inspection via spyware apps and external scanning devices. Policing contractors were also responsible for monitoring face-scanning machines and metal detectors at fixed checkpoints. All of these activities assured that Muslim residents continued to build the dataset of the system, making extremism assessment algorithms more and more precise. They were building a new ethno-racial variation of what the scholar Sareeta Amrute refers to as "race-as-algorithm"—turning Turkic Muslim social life into lines of code matched to a dataset of "pre-criminal" behaviors. Muslims who were determined to be "untrustworthy" through data checks were sent to detention centers where they were interrogated, asked to confess their pre-crime violations, and to name others who were also "untrustworthy."

The town of Qitai is 370 kilometers directly east of Shawan. One of the police contractors who conducted checks in Qitai was a young Kazakh man named Baimurat. He was in one of the first groups of contractors hired from across the region in late 2016. In an interview conducted with the Kazakh advocacy organization Ata Jurt after he fled across the border to Kazakhstan, he said that, because he was a college graduate, he was "considered very well qualified." As a result, he was given the highest-level salary available to contractors, around $1,000 per month, which is far above the minimum wage of around $300. Others in his cohort, who were considered less qualified because of their educational background, were paid closer to $400. For Baimurat, who had struggled to find work for which he was qualified in the past, taking the job was a choice he felt he could not refuse. Not only would he be able to provide for his family, but he would also be able to protect them from the reeducation system. "We were given uniforms," he said. "Then we started doing different kinds of training. It was really strict, as if we were planning for a war."

As part of the process of purging the regional administration of so-called "two faced" people—those who secretly show mercy and support to Muslims while publicly supporting the Party, Qitai authorities replaced key leaders with loyal state employees from other parts of China. The county police chief of Qitai was replaced with a new police commander, a Han man named Hua Chenzu from the eastern province of Fujian—the same locality that the regional government had placed in charge of transforming the local education system and building an industrial park in the county, which would put Uyghurs and Kazakhs to work under forced-labor contracts. In a state media story that highlights the biography and heroism of the new commander's fight to "eradicate evil," he is shown standing in an interrogation room next to a "tiger chair"—a torture device that immobilizes suspects.

Local authorities started building the People's Convenience Police Stations, where Vera would see herself on-screen. These surveillance hubs were built every several hundred meters in Muslim-majority areas as part of the Safe City grid. Then the authorities divided the contractors up and stationed them at one of the ninety-two stations that were built in Qitai County. In Shawan, a similar process played out in seventy-seven stations.

"We had to sit there monitoring the screens all the time," Baimurat recalled. "If we failed to notice an alert or stopped

56   looking, we would be punished." Over time, the kind of surveillance labor they did began to shift. First, the contractors were
sorted based on their Chinese language ability and other proofs
of their loyalty. "They made us do other exercises like reciting
rules about participating in the camp system," Baimurat said.
"We had to recite things related to law. There were quotes from
Xi Jinping on the walls of the station. We had to learn these by
heart. We were not allowed to go outside for the patrol until we
successfully recited them.

"After I worked there for six months, they handed out
devices to check pedestrians and car drivers," Baimurat remembered. "When we scanned their ID card [and phone] with it, we
got information about whether or not the person had worn a
veil, had installed WhatsApp, had traveled to Kazakhstan. All
sorts of things like that."

They began to perform night checks. The devices would
flash red if the person should be detained. "We could stop any
car we wanted on the street and check them. When we stopped
them, we asked the people inside to show their phones and
ID cards. If there was something suspicious like I mentioned
before, we needed to inform [the leaders]."

Initially, Baimurat and his coworkers felt that despite the
long hours and the confrontational positions they were placed
in, being a police contractor "was a good job" with a steady pay-
check and protection from police harassment. They saw themselves as on the side of the "good guys." This began to change
around the time that they received the smartphone scanning
equipment and Baimurat learned that the Kazakh middle school
had been turned into a prison. "They built an iron gate, high electric fence, and four watchtowers around the Kazakh school," he

recalled. "If we found anyone suspicious through the ID checks, they would send them to the Kazakh school. They had suddenly turned it into a prison. They forced all of the people who had been visiting mosques, praying, or wearing headscarves to go to that school."

Baimurat was officially a contingent worker hired on a contract basis. But six months into the new job, he learned he was not free to quit. "If we were tired and wanted to quit, they would tell us: *If you are exhausted, you can take a rest, but then you must come back. If you quit the job, then you will end up in the 'reeducation camps' too.*" When he saw what happened inside the camps for the first time, he understood what this threat actually meant.

"While I was working one day in early 2018, we had a meeting where we were told we had to transfer some detainees from the jail to the school," he said quietly. "We had so many manacles. When we got there, we saw that they had caught around six hundred people. There were rooms inside the building that were like cells. I saw very young women, very old women, and men with beards (over the age of fifty-five) among the detainees. They were all minorities, the majority were Uyghurs, then a few Kazakhs and some Hui people. I don't think there were Han people. Maybe one or two, but not more than that.

"We handcuffed and shackled them and then we gave blankets to them whether they could hold them or not, and we told them to get on the bus. I had to handcuff one person that I had a feeling I had seen before. Then I realized he had worked as a police contractor as well. I had seen him before while I was working. I didn't remember his name, but I knew him. I really wanted to ask what happened to him, but because there were

58   cameras, I didn't ask any questions. I thought maybe I could ask him later. But I never found a chance.

"Then we started transporting women. I suddenly heard really sharp screams. I saw an old woman in her eighties whose hair was completely white. She screamed when she was shackled and handcuffed because her leg was injured. They just dragged her to the bus. When I witnessed this, I felt terribly bad. I wanted to quit. I regretted being a police [officer] with every fiber of my being. I was crying on the inside." As he said this, Baimurat touched his hand to his chest.

Sometime later, when he felt it was safe, he asked another Kazakh police contractor about the man he had recognized. His coworker told him that the man came from a village and didn't understand how the CCTV cameras worked. While he was working in the prison, he saw a piece of paper on the floor with the words *get me out of here* written on it. He didn't report the incident, but the cameras saw it, so he was taken "to study." Baimurat realized that any Kazakh or Uyghur could be sent to the camps. No one was safe from the surveillance system, no matter how hard they tried. "I felt very bad about being part of the system. There were so many people who made very tiny mistakes and ended up in the camps. As police, we had tasks we must fulfill. Some days the leaders said do this, other days they said do that. Each day we had to do what they said."

Over time, the pressure wore on Baimurat. "We couldn't sleep," he said, shaking his head. "We were crying all the time, me and my wife. But we didn't show other people that we were crying, because they might think we were dangerous and might inform on us."

Safe City   59

Back in Shawan, as the Safe City project was implemented, a similar process unfolded. On the weekend of April 7, 2017, the leaders of Shawan County attended a meeting where Chen Quanguo declared a new beginning to the ongoing "de-extremification" campaign. The cadres said that they would renew their resolve to "resolutely oppose the infiltration of religious extremist ideas." By August 2017, the county jail had been expanded and officially turned into a "centralized closed education training center." By the end of 2019, a detention facility that could house more than seven thousand people had been built.

Since 2017, the Xinjiang Victims Database has documented more than a hundred testimonies from former Shawan detainees and the families of current detainees and prisoners. In some cases, they said they were detained because they had passports or had used illegal apps. Visiting mosques too frequently— the location of the majority of face recognition cameras installed in Shawan's Safe City project—was the reason that was most often given.

In the Shawan study, the assessors argued that the project would "greatly improve the local government's ability to quickly respond to major events and ensure economic construction." At the same time, they suggested it would also foster private business investment and improve social security by protecting private property. "The indirect economic benefits are immeasurable," they wrote.

In April 2017, months after the new "round up those who should be rounded up" campaign was established and the assessors filed their report, the Party Secretary of Tacheng Prefecture, a man named Xue Bing, visited Shawan and toured the different

60 facilities involved in the campaign. He visited the Public Security Bureau command center to inspect the new Safe City system. He discussed strengthening "education and management services" for mosques and religious leaders. He placed an emphasis on "study transfer" programs and that cadres tasked with village surveillance should fully embrace their role in waving the "assessment baton . . . and enforce strict discipline in the villages."

Shawan and Kuitun are both small towns. When I visited them in 2015, I was struck by how uniformly generic each appeared. All were made up of gray concrete tenement buildings built on a grid that centered around a town square, a market, and a train station. Everyone knew each other. They would certainly know if camps were built on the edge of town and several thousand Muslims disappeared into them. They would also know if a new industrial park was built and still more Muslims were forced to work there. And they would notice if dozens of surveillance hubs were built and everyone had to have their face scanned. All of this was as obvious as the five fingers on my hand, as a saying in Uyghur goes.

As in every county across the region, the Safe City project enveloped Shawan. From the apps on their phones, to the entrances to their homes, to mosques and train stations, the lives of Shawan residents were made visible and were organized by digital codes that matched their faces. These codes were flexible systems of enclosure and surveillance—they could be turned on and off and their sensitivity could be manually adjusted. They circulated only on the regional intranet among police contractors who were themselves surveilled by the system.

As the Shawan study noted, the surveillance system centered on assuring the movement of "beneficial" goods, services, and biometric data, while channeling or stopping the movement of objects, bodies, and data that could potentially disrupt this circulation. The goal was to increase the circulation of what was deemed "good" within a state-supported market economy while decreasing the circulation of that which was deemed "bad" such as crime and unassimilable bodies. The shaping power of this technology was used to regulate the population to produce lower rates of fear among non-Muslims and higher rates of economic growth and greater power for the authorities. For people like Qeyser's family and low-level data janitors like Baimurat who feared that they could accidently trigger the system or that someone could flip the switch to target them at any time, the Safe City produced the inverse effect: deep fear and radical disempowerment. It turned the convenience of smartphones into a disaster.

In the control society of a Safe City, life is made predictable by maintaining relations of power at a technical remove. It does something more than this too. When the technology begins to think for people, it starts to normalize its power over life. When space for thinking is lost in the black box of a complex automatic system, it becomes banal and inhumane, producing profound capacities for cruelty.

Two Faced

In February 2017, as the reeducation camp system swung into motion and Baimurat began his work as a contractor, school-teachers from across the region were pressed into service as camp instructors. One of these instructors was a Muslim woman named Qelbinur Sedik, who taught Chinese to fifth graders in a primary school in Ürümchi. The daughter of Uyghur and Uzbek government officials, Qelbinur's parents recognized the relative protection of being identified as a non-Uyghur, so they registered her as an Uzbek on her birth certificate. As a minority who had been educated in Chinese in the 1980s, Qelbinur was pushed toward a career in education. After graduating from the regional teacher's college in 1992, she took up a post at a primary school in Ürümchi.

Because she held a senior position at the school, she was surprised when she received a new assignment after the 2017 break for the Spring Festival. "On February 26, 2017, we started a new semester," she recalled. "The principal called me to his office and told me that I needed to go to a meeting," said

Qelbinur. In the meeting, the secretary of the district party office didn't offer much detail. Qelbinur and the other teachers in the meeting were just told that the authorities had gathered a group of "uneducated people." It was their responsibility to teach them Chinese. The group of "uneducated people" were in a government office building up on the mountain. Qelbinur was told that she had to sign a "letter of commitment" that said she would teach them for six months. Then they gave her another document that stated she must be willing "to take all responsibility and the requisite punishment" if she said anything about what she observed. "They emphasized that this was a political assignment and that we could not refuse or ask to leave," she recalled. "Otherwise, we would be punished." Qelbinur did not need to say anything about the meeting to anyone at her school. It seemed like everyone higher in command knew what the assignment was all about. "The next day when I left the school, my teaching responsibilities had been assigned to other people."

Qelbinur, like nearly all Uyghurs throughout the region, had in fact already heard about what she referred to as "uneducated, migrant" Uyghurs who had been sent to reeducation camps as early as 2015. When she first heard about them, she thought it sounded terrible, but that it had little to do with her, an urban Chinese-speaking woman with a secure Uzbek identification. As she prepared for the new assignment, Qelbinur remembered what a woman from Awat County in Aksu Prefecture, a county near Qeyser's home village in rural southern Xinjiang, had told her. The woman, one of the teachers in the primary school, had moved to Ürümchi after graduating from school. She went back to her home village every summer vacation.

64   In 2015, when the woman had come back to the city, she had been very sad and cried in the office for two hours. "She told me, 'People who prayed regularly, who wore long dresses, or who were imams, were being detained,'" Qelbinur remembered. "Awat is a big county, and has one of the largest Uyghur populations. 'But,' she said, 'you won't find any male Uyghurs on the streets anymore.'"

Her colleague's three older brothers were all taken. One brother was taken because he was devout in his Islamic practice, one was taken because someone accused him of going to Friday prayers at a mosque, and the third was taken for some unknown reason. "They gathered all of them in a big hall," she told Qelbinur. "The police were carrying weapons. People's names were called, their crimes were declared, and a sentence was given. Police then took that person away with a black plastic bag over their head." Thinking about this years later, Qelbinur recalled, "When she said this, we all cried with her."

Yet she also remembered that life soon seemed to go back to normal. "We felt a shock, but over time I forgot about this conversation. I thought Ürümchi would never be like that." But when the officials said that she was being assigned to teach a "group of uneducated people," that story her colleague had told came flooding back. "I thought it must be something similar because they kept saying over and over that it was a political assignment and that we were not allowed to tell anyone about it," she remembered. "So I wondered if I was going to the kind of place that my colleague mentioned before, but I tried to push this thought out of my mind."

The next day, with a sick feeling in her stomach, Qelbinur was taken to what she saw was a "centralized controlled education

training center." It was clear that the government buildings that
had been refitted as a "smart" camp were exactly like what her
colleague had described.

"When I arrived at the building, I felt I had come to a
prison. It was a four-story building surrounded by razor wire.
We entered the gate by swiping our ID card. When we passed
through the grounds of the compound, I felt very nervous. The
yard was guarded by Han police officers and soldiers with assault
rifles." Qelbinur recalled thinking, "I have to be very careful and
make a good impression on them."

It was a lot to absorb. Time seemed both to speed up and
slow down, but images from that day are seared in her mind.
"After I finished registering, I remember looking around and
noticing a slogan on the wall that said *Fight against religious
extremism thoughts, and prevent the entrance of religious ideas.*"

It took her some time to fully understand the layout of the
compound, but when she re-creates it in her mind now, she can
picture each room vividly. "When I entered the building, on the
right, there were four police officers and a stair to the second
floor," she told me. "On the left, there were seven or eight offices.
Among them was a police command center, a dorm room for
police, a nurse's medical office, and an office for staff from the
neighborhood watch units."

This detail was significant, because it made clear to her that
the Civil Affairs Ministry, a branch of the Chinese government
that implements social services and supports the police, was
actually in charge of monitoring the progress of the detainees.
"Ten young women from the neighborhood watch units came
to assist in the camp work in shifts," Qelbinur told me. "After
five of them finished a shift, another five would take over their

66   responsibilities. Their responsibilities included dispensing steamed buns to the detainees and documenting their behavior for the detainees' digital files."

As Qelbinur took in the atmosphere of the reeducation camp, her own role as a camp worker began. Other Muslim workers in the camp began to show her how to perform to the standards of the system. "A police officer brought me to their office," she remembered. "There I met an Uyghur officer named Mahira. She told me that she knew me, that her child was a student at my school. I wanted to ask for more information about the camp from this woman, but she implied that I should not ask for more. She simply said, 'Look up.' And I found that there were cameras pointed at my face. I understood and didn't ask anything further. She asked, 'Are you ready to start the class?' Feeling I didn't have any choice, I said, 'Yes.'"

Armed with the knowledge that her behavior was being watched by the "smart" cameras of the camp, Qelbinur crossed a threshold that would change her life. "I took my books and water bottle, stared at the iron door, and saw something that I will never forget for the rest of my life. The door was opened and the detainees started coming out wearing handcuffs. They had to duck under a chain that held the door partially closed. They walked to the classroom. When I saw them, I could not help but to have tears in my eyes." While the "students" sat on the plastic stools, Qelbinur was given a table, chair, and blackboard to use.

"When I saw their faces, I felt crushed," Qelbinur told me. "I prayed to Allah to keep me from crying in front of them. I came to the table in the front without knowing what to do and what to say. Among the people sitting in front of me were elderly men with beards. They looked respectable, just like the

kind of elderly people you might see in the mosque." As a Turkic
Muslim who had been taught her whole life to respect her elders,
Qelbinur was confronted with a choice: put on the mask of the
Chinese-speaking reeducation system, which showed "absolutely no mercy," or reveal her truer self as someone who was
taught to treat others with dignity and respect and risk being
labeled "two faced"—the threat that hung over all Muslims
since their loyalty to the state was always in question.

"Without thinking, I said, 'Assalamu alaykum,'" a common
Arabic-origin greeting meaning: "Peace be upon you." When she
said this, the students froze. "They looked terrified. I realized I
had said something wrong. I introduced myself and started the
class. I just stared at the blackboard, and didn't turn back to look
at their faces. I couldn't turn around because some detainees
were sobbing. Some of the old men's beards were wet from
crying. I tried to compose myself. I didn't look back at all during
the class. I just kept writing and erasing the characters on the
blackboard. I finished four different classes, but I felt like it took
four years."

In this encounter, Qelbinur was unable to face the detainees,
to witness the immediacy of their suffering directly. Yet, because
of her initial identification with them—through the enunciation
of a banned Arabic phrase, and her lack of composure, even with
her back turned to the detainees—it was clear to the detainees
that she recognized them as human, as deserving of empathy. In
that moment of exposure, her reeducation mask fell away and
she was seen as a two faced Muslim.

"When I went to the office during the break, Mahira told me
that I should be careful about what I said. She said I should say
only 'Hello students' (*xueyuanmen hao*) in Chinese. I went out

68   into the grounds of the compound. There was no camera there. The director of the camp was an Uyghur man named Kadir. He was tall and tan. He said, 'You need to be careful about what you say. You shouldn't say *assalamu alaykum*. Saying that can be considered a crime and you might be detained for saying that. Luckily, today it is me and two other police on duty.'"

Kadir's recognition of the difficulty of the reeducation task and their shared Muslim identification gave Qelbinur courage to ask a bit more about the detainees.

"I asked, 'Who are those people?'"

"He said, 'They are imams and people who worked in the mosques.'"

"I said, 'I will be careful next time.'"

"He said again, 'You are lucky this time, because I was in the camera room.'"

"I asked, 'When were those students taken in here?'"

"He replied, 'On February 14.'"

"I asked, 'Did they commit any crimes?'"

"He replied, 'No. They are just religious Uyghurs. You need to be careful. Right above your head in the classroom, there are four cameras.'"

In his responses, Kadir pushed Qelbinur to recognize the detainees as different from them, as religious and thus deserving of punishment. Over and over he emphasized the way the system pushed them to show no recognition of the dehumanization of other Turkic Muslims.

Qelbinur made it through this first day of work in the camp in a daze. At the end of the day, the police dropped her off somewhere in the city and she rode buses for hours to find her way home. "My husband was at home and he asked me about my day in the reeducation center," she remembered. "He asked, 'Who were the students?' I cried so hard and explained everything to him. My husband was shocked. I asked him to keep it a secret. Until now, none of my relatives know."

Qelbinur began to acclimate to the stress of performing in front of the cameras. One day after she finished one of her classes, a detainee who was around forty asked if they could stay for another hour. "I asked 'Why?' and he said, 'It is better for us to stay in the classroom.' I understood what he meant." She had glimpsed the inside of their cell, which at that point, before bright lights were installed, was very dimly lit and had a bare concrete floor. The detainees could sit on stools in the class-room, but in their cells they sat pressed up against each other on the concrete floor for many hours at a time. They were not per-mitted to stand or lie down without permission.

Qelbinur did not respond to the man, and camp guards immediately came to take him away. "They knew that if they talked, they would be punished," Qelbinur said. The next week the young man did not come to class, and she never saw him again. After that incident, the others in the class never spoke except to answer questions about the class in Chinese.

It became increasingly clear to her that a process of dehuman-ization was unfolding in the camp. Within a week, the detainees had their heads shaved. Several weeks later, the classrooms became cells to accommodate hundreds of new detainees. There were so many detainees that they had to take turns sleeping on the concrete floor. The detainees were deeply fearful. Their voices trembled when they answered questions in class.

At this point in the interview, Qelbinur was sobbing, wiping at her face with her hand. "They were all so scared. When I asked

70   something during class, they would not look at my face. At first, there was life on their faces. But after one week, the beards and hair of the men were shaved. At first the female detainees had long hair, but after one week, it was shaved. There was no energy in their eyes. I did not want to look at them. Because every time I looked at them, I could not help but be sad. At night, I couldn't sleep. The sound of the iron chains was still ringing in my ears when I tried."

Over time, the violence she was forced to support and enact affected not just her body but her sense of self. Although she attempted to hide this beneath a veneer of "trustworthiness," eventually this became impossible. The violence of functioning within the camp system wore her down. Violating the person-hood of others resulted in a violation of her own sense of dignity and self-worth. As the anthropologists Nancy Scheper-Hughes and Philip Bourgois note, "Violence can never be understood solely in terms of its physicality—force, assault, or the inflic-tion of pain—alone. The social and cultural dimensions of vio-lence are what gives violence its power and meaning."

In contemporary Northwest China, Muslims are stopped, identified, detained, and interrogated by state proxies on a daily basis. Most often these encounters are brief, with very few words exchanged. Instead, the digital history contained in their smartphone and the biometric tracking space speaks for them. If this "speech" is flagged by the system, it may result in more formal interrogation at a People's Convenience Police Station or higher-level precinct.

This questioning happens elsewhere too. On Mondays, their political knowledge and loyalty is examined at flag-raising ceremonies and interactive political education sessions. At work their behavior is observed, tasks are asked of them. They are always on guard. These processes result in a second, politically engaged sense of interrogation through which they internalize the way they are at the mercy of police contractors and their coworkers.

Writing about ethnoracial minorities and policing in France, Didier Fassin notes, "They understand that it is not enough to be innocent in order not to be deemed guilty. . . . They become aware that what is happening to them is related not to what they have done, but to what they represent." It is through this process of subjection that Turkic Muslims understand that in a time of reeducation they are subject to the gaze of the system. Anyone can be an informant; no one is a guaranteed ally; and the algorithms of cameras and scanners are always on. In this context, for ethnoracial minorities, there appears to be no space that is fully outside state power. This is confirmed on a daily basis by the checkpoints and the fears of their relatives, neighbors, and friends. Ultimately, for Muslims who are assigned to work within the system, it is confirmed by the treatment of those who have been deemed "untrustworthy." The dehumanizing effects of the camps and social and technological conditions that surround them make clear that any Muslim can be detainable. Seeing this ordinary state violence enacted on a daily basis drives home the point that dehumanization is not random, but is in fact related to what Muslims represent.

At the same time that Muslims such as Qelbinur and Baimurat were always potentially untrustworthy, their Han colleagues did not appear to feel a level of danger to the same degree. For Qelbinur this was made clear one day when she saw a young female detainee rushed away in a stretcher, her face

72 ghostly pale. When Qelbinur took the bus home that night, a Han camp worker who taught law at the camp accompanied her for part of the journey. In the relative safety of the back of the bus, the teacher turned to her and asked in a low voice if she had seen the young woman too. "I said yes but that I didn't know what was going on," Qelbinur recalled. "He told me, 'That woman had a massive hemorrhage and passed away on the way to the hospital.'" Like all the women in the camp, she had been forced to take a pill to stop her menstrual cycle. "Women in the camp have to take the pill to stop them from having their period because the school can't provide them with enough pads," he stated plainly.

Qelbinur did not know how to respond. She knew that this was not the full truth. Across the entire region, the Civil Affairs Ministry had embarked on a "Zero Illegal Births" campaign. She herself, at age forty-seven, was forced to have regular inspections of a new IUD that state workers had forced her to implant. State documents show that women of childbearing age who did not submit to surgical sterilization or IUD implantation and regular inspections would not be added to the list of "trustworthy" citizens. Illegal pregnancies were to be "disposed of early"—a reference to forced abortions. The Civil Affairs Ministry began to give rewards of up to almost $1,000 to anyone who reported violations of family planning regulations. Other state documents show that a significant portion of people sent to the camps, perhaps as many as 10 percent of all detainees, were sent due to violations of family planning regulations. Since the camp system began, in some areas of Southern Xinjiang, birth rates among Uyghurs have plummeted by between 50 and 80 percent due in part to these restrictions on Muslim reproductive rights.

But, during the bus ride, Qelbinur did not know if she could
trust her Han coworker so she just nodded to say she understood. "I kept silent, but I was suffering on the inside. He just
kept complaining." He told her, "What kind of a 'school' is this?
Many of our 'students' are well educated. They have studied
abroad in places like South Korea, the United States, Egypt,
Canada, Turkey, Japan, and Kazakhstan. I don't even have the
ability to answer their questions. Isn't this the twenty-first
century? How can this be happening now?' He was so angry."
Qelbinur just remained silent, surprised that he was alluding
so openly to past world historical events when camps had been
used as part of eugenics campaigns. Over the rest of her time
working in the camp, they never spoke about their shared horror
again. They just continued to do what they were told.

In fact, many Han people who were involved in the reeducation system appeared to develop a sense of empowerment
and investment in the campaign. Qelbinur recalled another Han
coworker, forgetting that Qelbinur was half-Uyghur herself,
telling her, "Right now, Uyghurs are like flies. We can just swat
them if we like." One of her former students told her that, when
his brother was taken by a group of armed police in the middle of
the night, a group of Han neighbors gathered in the hall outside
his apartment and applauded. "He told me they shouted, *Excellent work!* and *Please take them all away!*" The student asked her,
"Teacher, you always said all the ethnic groups should be uni-
fied and harmonious. Why would they applaud when a Uyghur
was taken?" Because there was a camera in location where they
were speaking, Qelbinur felt compelled to tell her student, "No,
you must not have heard what they were saying correctly. They
wouldn't do that. Maybe your brother is going somewhere to

74   receive an education." Qelbinur remembered feeling helpless as the ten-year-old sobbed and said through his tears, "Don't lie to me. How could he go to school with a black bag over his head? Why would the police take him like that if they saw him as a student? I'm young, but I'm not stupid."

Since the People's War on Terror began in 2014, Han citizens often generally supported the system. In a 2020 interview, a Han migrant to the region named Kong Yuanfeng told me, "Because they were detaining so many people, a lot of Han migrants who didn't really know anything about Uyghurs thought that the terrorists must be everywhere."

Others complained because the security systems disrupted some forms of commerce and construction. In a 2019 interview, another Han woman from Xinjiang, Lu Yin, told me that, at first, when the campaign began in 2017, her relatives complained about the checkpoints. They told her that they thought it was intolerable when everyone who was riding a public bus to the city had to wait while the Uyghurs were checked. After several months, "It got better," because the buses just started leaving the Uyghurs behind at the checkpoints while Han continued on to the city.

"What was most striking to me was the way [my relatives] had become so expressively racist," Lu told me. "Around 75 percent of the time, the topic of their conversation was denigrating Uyghurs." Lu Yin said this was particularly alarming because, "When I visited in 2016, these [casual racist comments] only came up two or three times per day. Now it was something people brought up twenty or thirty times per day." Whenever there was a lull in conversation, her relatives and their neighbors would exclaim, "Uyghurs are so bad!" And then begin to talk about how backward, ungrateful, and violent they were. Over the course of the weeks she was there, she felt as though "they were trying to justify what was happening [to her]." She heard them say that the government had no choice but to intervene in the situation. They told her Uyghurs were much "worse" than the African Americans they saw on TV during the Black Lives Matter protests, so this is why the camps and "reeducation" work were necessary.

The primary reservations Han people had in participating in the reeducation campaign was having to sacrifice significant portions of their lives to this effort. Those who were sent to monitor Uyghurs and Kazakhs in villages complained about having to adjust to new conditions. The work was boring and they missed the excitement of city life. They missed their families. They wanted to get back to their work as bureaucrats in state-owned enterprises and government bureaus, or their work as doctors and editors in state-run institutions. Two of those I interviewed told me that they or their friends who had been asked to go down to the villages would have lost their jobs if they had refused to participate in the monitoring program, but they also said that by participating they had been guaranteed promotions upon the completion of their tours of duty. In many cases, though, they just accepted the assignments. They felt that working in the system was part of what it meant to be a good citizen.

Qelbinur said that she felt like the "evil" of the system had seeped into the Han population as a whole and had even begun to infect her. At times she felt numb to the pain she saw on a daily basis. But then, months into her assignment, another moment reminded her how the dehumanization of Muslims had been made normal. As she was riding a bus through a neighborhood

76 on the south side of Ürümchi, some Han teenagers leaned out of the bus windows in front of her and yelled at several Uyghurs who they saw on the side of the street, "Why are you still here?" As the bus rumbled past them, they turned to each other and began to discuss why some of the Uyghurs in that neighborhood hadn't been taken away yet. Qelbinur looked down at her feet and said nothing. "I couldn't say anything, because I knew they were right. They could have had me taken away if they had wanted to. They had been given that power."

Smart Camps

Technologies have played an important role in the history of population control, ranging from the razor wire and automatic weapons of North American internment camps to the passbooks and checkpoints of Apartheid South Africa. As historian Ann Stoler has shown, in colonial contexts, techniques of classifying behavior have the effect of normalizing relationships of domination in more and more intimate ways. The technology used in "smart" surveillance systems to contain and transform Muslim populations in Northwest China takes these systems of control to new levels of scale and intensity. Technologies produce distance between cause and effect. This can mask or enhance their effects. Like science itself, they offer limited truth claims that people are often willing to accept as the norm. Taken together, they accelerate processes of dehumanization.

Part of what extended the banality of the system in the camps was the omnipresence of guards, automated cameras, and voice recognition technology. In one of my long interviews with Qelbinur, she recalled how, on the very first day when she entered the camp, she was surprised by the police presence and high levels of technological security. "I was surprised that there were so many police armed with guns. This was actually the first indication I had that it was not a regular school," she remembered. "There were so many police sitting in the front hall ready to respond to any incident. They had just told me that I was going to teach a group of uneducated people, so at first I thought maybe they were there to protect the students with their guns."

It was only when a government worker opened one of the cell doors and told the detainees to go to the classroom that Qelbinur realized that the people were detained and that she was in a camp. Each detainee was wearing handcuffs. "I realized then that there was a huge difference between what the internal documents said about 'training centers' and the reality of the camps. The camps were unimaginable," Qelbinur told me. The internal directives from the head of security for the region, Zhu Hailun, said that the guards should not carry lethal weapons, but Qelbinur said many of them carried guns even inside the camp enclosures. The directives said that hygiene was a major concern, but Qelbinur saw that basic sanitation was neglected. The directives said nothing about beating and torturing "students" who were unable to tell the guards what they wanted to hear, but Qelbinur observed this on a regular basis.

The camps were designed to use technological control to create a false reality about what happened in the camps. This was apparent in the way camp guards examined Qelbinur's phone. "Before we arrived at the camp, the police told us to turn off our phones," she remembered. "Under no circumstances were we to answer our phones or make a call. When we arrived, they forced us to put our phones in the staff office. We were only permitted to use our phone again after we left the camp."

It became a normal routine: Every morning when the police picked her up to take her to the camp she would power off her phone. Only on one occasion did they plug her phone into a device like the one Baimurat had used in Qitai. "They just inserted the cable into it and then gave the phone back to me. I didn't ask anything. I just gave them my ID card like the others. They scanned this too."

When she was in the camp, Qelbinur was always conscious of the cameras. She said, "In the classroom there were four cameras in the front, two in the middle, and four in the back. Even though the light was not that bright, it seemed they could watch everything we did." One day the tall Uyghur camp administrator named Kadir gave her a tour of the "command center." It consisted of banks of TV monitors, a console with many buttons, a joystick, and a microphone. Four guards worked in shifts around the clock to watch the screens. If the detainees got up from the floor or spoke, "They yelled at the detainees. They yelled whenever they made a move: *Don't talk! Don't speak Uyghur!*" Even in low light, faces could be seen in high definition. This stood out to her as something that was quite astonishing. Even in cells crowded with so many people they had to sleep in shifts, every face appeared on the screen like in a WeChat video call, except they were clearer. If anyone moved, their motion was automatically detected. "When they made any gesture, the camera captured that. For example, if anyone talks to others, even in the middle of the night, the guards would yell at them over the intercom," she remembered. What was even more startling was the way "the police could click on that person's face to make it bigger on the screen." They could pull up the detainee's name and number in an instant. You could also use the system to search for particular detainees or groups. "For example, if you want to check the number 10 cell, you just click 10," she said.

What Qelbinur saw was the command center of a "smart camp" system—a facility that the tech firm Dahua says is supported by technologies such as "computer vision systems, big data analytics and cloud computing." According to the manual approved by Zhu Hailun, the camps were to "perfect peripheral isolation, internal separation, protective defenses, safe passageways, and other facilities and equipment, and ensure that security instruments, security equipment, video surveillance, one-button alarms, and other such devices are in place and functioning." This "smart" camp scheme resonates with regional Party Secretary Chen Quanguo's vision that the camps should "teach like a school, be managed like the military, and be defended like a prison."

According to documents from the private prison contractor Lonbon, face recognition and so-called "emotion or affect recognition" technologies have been installed throughout the Uyghur region prison system. The system Qelbinur described seeing in her camp in Ürümchi meets much of the parameters of the Lonbon and Dahua systems. In their most elaborated forms, such systems proport to monitor the emotional states of prisoners using constant assessments of facial expressions through high-definition video cameras. The systems are designed to "eliminate the ideological problems of prisoners" by alternating between "mandatory interruptions" that correspond to the supposed mental states of prisoners and cultural programing that ensures "the thought change is carried out in a subtle way."

In addition to the "smart" surveillance, the camp also had all of the trappings of a high security prison. "From the outside, no

80 one would know for sure that it was a camp," she recalled. "You would only realize it was a camp when you entered the compound. When you entered the building, you would know with absolute certainty that it was camp. There was an iron mesh fence at each intermediate stair landing between each floor." She recalled thinking that not even a mosquito could escape the enclosure. "It looked like the type of prison used to detain dangerous criminals, like I had seen in American movies."

It was not just the sights that told her it was a camp. Or even the sounds of chains, the resounding clang of metal doors. Or even the chanting of Chinese and patriotic songs from the classrooms. Those sounds continue to haunt her, but it was the sounds she heard from the interrogation rooms that conveyed the full horrific cruelty of the camp. "Sometimes we could hear the screaming of the detainees at the first camp," she said, a look of pain on her face. "I asked Director Kadir what kind of method they were using to interrogate detainees. He said there was a tiger chair and an electronic hat and gloves. During lunchtime, I could hear the screaming."

Two Faced
In the context of the Xinjiang reeducation system, Turkic Muslim police contractors and camp instructors are often treated as though they are simultaneously essential and disposable; trustworthy and untrustworthy. Neither Baimurat nor Qelbinur were permitted to step away from their roles in the system without considerable costs to themselves. The threat of being labeled "two faced" always hung over them. They said that being placed in this position produced an unbearable strain on their lives. Due to her depression, lack of sleep, and appetite,

Qelbinur's blood pressure dropped to dangerously low levels. She contemplated suicide. She kept pills beside her pillow to swallow quickly if the police came in the middle of the night. Unable to walk, and fearing that she might have a stroke, she was admitted to a hospital. Baimurat felt a similar strain. Unable to sleep at night, he and his fellow police-contractors began to drink liquor even while on duty as a way of coping.

Eventually, Baimurat was able to leverage his Kazakh-stani citizenship and the threat of international attention to renounce his Chinese citizenship and flee to Kazakhstan with the assistance of Kazakhstani government officials. Because of her ill health, Qelbinur was allowed to retire. Due, she thinks, to a bureaucratic oversight, she had her passport returned to her and was allowed to visit her daughter in Europe. Prior to these institutional interventions in their lives, they were told over and over by authorities that they would be detained if they refused to participate in the camps system.

Many of the moments from their time in the camps continue to play over and over in Baimurat's and Qelbinur's minds. When at last they were in a protected space, Baimurat and Qelbinur felt as though they had no choice but to tell people about what they had been forced to participate in.

It was the moments when they recognized themselves as perpetrators or as having to be untrue to their own sense of dignity that stood out the most to them—the moments when they had to prove that they were not "two faced." For Baimurat, the true gravity of his work as a contractor in placing people in camps came when he saw lines of Uyghur and Kazakh women, including the elderly and infirm, being loaded onto buses. When he saw his coworkers and family members shackled and taken

82   away, he fully realized that his body, too, could be targeted by the reeducation system. Likewise, when Qelbinur recognized that she was playing a role in the dehumanization of other Turkic Muslims, she was forced to turn away and sob even as the cameras recorded her emotional response. While it was possible for them to hide behind a "trustworthy" mask in their role as police assistant and teacher at times, they could never fully escape their Muslim identities. Their life stories and the Turkic phenotypes of their faces proceeded before them—their ethnicity always placed them in a racialized category of suspicion.

These moments of recognition resonate with a moment described in the 1960s by social theorist Frantz Fanon in which a white French child pointed to Fanon, an eloquent French speaker and psychiatrist, and declared, "Look, a Negro!" In his analysis of this moment, Fanon shows how racialization is enacted through assessments of ethno-racial difference itself. An ethno-racialized colonial gaze fixes the identity of the phenotypes and culture of the other, making it something that cannot be overcome as long as a colonial power structure remains in place. No matter how well the colonized speaks the language of the colonizer, which Fanon refers to as a "white mask" in the French colonial context, the colonized will always be recognized as lacking and potentially other—a "two faced" person. Even if the colonized attempts to escape the association of the colonized by mimicking the colonizer and thinking of themselves as unmarked subjects entitled to police and legal protections, these protections can be taken away at a moment's notice. For Baimurat and Qelbinur, the mask of reeducated "trustworthiness" slipped away when they saw themselves reflected in the eyes of their former coworkers and neighbors.

In his consideration of Fanon's decolonial framework in the context of colonial India, Homi Bhabha examines the way colonial powers develop intricate strategies of domination. He found that a class of interpreters was essential to such systems. In the logic of such systems, the class of interpreters who moved between the colonized subaltern and the colonial officials would adopt the forms of cultural distinction and values of the colonizer. Yet, as Bhabha shows, the hybrid figure of the interpreter is never able to fully inhabit this role. Instead, the interpreter remains an ambivalent figure. As permitted versions of otherness, they produce what Bhabha refers to as an always "partial vision of the colonizer's presence." Because of the ethno-racial trace that remains, these interpreters are destined to remain forever stuck in forms of mimicry, and subject to sudden denunciation at the slightest misstep.

Baimurat's and Qelbinur's stories are both normal and exceptional. While perhaps most, if not all, Turkic Muslim camp workers experienced similar moments of extreme stress, the vast majority of them have not been able to step outside of the system. Instead, they have remained embedded in the penal colony, unable to speak or even cry openly.

Both Baimurat and Qelbinur noted that, over time, certain aspects of violence in the camps became normal. It became more and more difficult to be surprised by what they saw. The normalization of dehumanizing violence appeared to be endemic within the camp system. But there were moments of exception.

Moments of shared experience are moments in which power is enacted. The profoundly negative experience of being hailed by the gaze of detainees demonstrates the power of a colonial state. At the same time, moments of active witnessing, of recognizing

84   the self in the other and sharing their pain, can also produce
forms of decolonial refusal. These types of moments changed
Baimurat's and Qelbinur's lives forever. As an ethnographer, it
is these types of moments that I pay attention to. Collecting and
translating them has the potential to shape the way the world
witnesses Turkic Muslim suffering. There is a Uyghur proverb
that describes this decolonial impulse well: "Drop by drop a lake
is formed" (Uy: *tama—tama köl bolar*).

A Uyghur woman I interviewed during a research trip to
Xinjiang in 2018 told me that many of the police contractors she
knew had contemplated suicide. Others told me that their relatives who worked inside the reeducation system often cried
when they came home at night. Qelbinur said that, after that
day crying at the blackboard with her back to the detainees,
it became impossible for her to eat steamed bread without
thinking about the way the detainees were starving. "When I
saw snow, I couldn't help but cry. Because I was thinking about
them. I was thinking about them freezing in their cold cells."

The Animals

In mid-2017, a Kazakh farmer named Adilbek returned to China from Kazakhstan where he and his wife and children had moved several months before. In order to finalize the move, he needed to round up a herd of around a hundred sheep that he had leased from the local work brigade. The day after he arrived in his home village near Wusu, around thirty kilometers from Vera's hometown, the local police came and took away his passport. He explained that he was just returning temporarily and would need a month or two to round up the brigade's sheep and complete the transfer of nearly two thousand acres of mountainous pastureland to its new owners. "I explained that my wife and children were already Kazakhstani citizens and that I was planning to become one too," Adilbek recalled. "I said I would come to get my passport when I was ready."

After he completed the livestock drive and his business dealings, Adilbek went back to the police station to ask for his passport. They told him he needed six stamps of approval from different offices in the bureaucracy. "So I went and got them,"

86   Adilbek said. "Then they said I need seven stamps. They said I
      had to start from the very beginning again. So I started doing this.
      Then they said there is no need for you to be involved. We will do
      it for you and call you when it is ready." By this time bureaucratic
      offices around the country were closed due to the Nineteenth
      Party Congress in Beijing, so the local authorities told Adilbek
      they would not work on his passport for another fifty days.

          On the surface, Adilbek appeared to be stuck in the red tape
      of the system. But Adilbek discovered that there was a more
      pernicious force at work. He was being slotted into an untrust-
      worthy "extremist" category. When the police were two stamps
      into recalling his passport again, they called him. They said that,
      to proceed, they needed to take him to the hospital for a health
      check. But something didn't seem right. They did not tell him
      he was under arrest, but they took his shoes away and gave him
      a pair of cloth ones that were missing shoelaces. "They didn't
      handcuff me, because I knew all of them. They had grown up
      with me."

          The health check passed in a blur—a prick in the finger,
      a voice recording, an iris scan—but then the police said they
      needed to stop by a school. "When we arrived at 'the school,'
      I saw that it had a thick black gate. They handcuffed me then,
      before entering the gate," he said.

          As soon as he saw the gate of the camp, he knew that some-
      thing was definitely wrong. "I was very scared at that point,"
      Adilbek remembered. He was changed into a gray track suit
      and a black hood was put over his head. "The police contrac-
      tors who took me there told me that I was going to be put in the
      camp. They asked me. 'What have you done? They gave us your
      name to take you there.' I didn't know what I was guilty of, so I

pled with them. No one knew why they were taking me there. I screamed as they dragged me into the dark."

In Uyghur and Kazakh conceptualizations of halal standards, animals that are being prepared for slaughter should not witness the death of other animals while they wait their turn. Instead, after a quick prayer of blessing, the death should be swift and unexpected, a quick slice of the throat. Adilbek felt as though this was how his neighbors prepared him for life behind "the black gate," a euphemism frequently used by Uyghurs and Kazakhs to refer to the camps. They did not want him to know what would come next. Maybe this was because they thought it would be easier to handle him this way. Maybe it was because they cared about him and wanted his social death to be swift. Adilbek will never know for sure. The levels of dehumanization Adilbek experienced over the next year were unimaginable to him. "We were treated worse than dogs," he said. His life, like those of more than a dozen other former detainees I interviewed, became a struggle to survive.

A Machine of Dehumanization

The first thing Adilbek noticed in what he called the "prison cell" where he spent his first six months of detention was that "the door was so thick." It had a hole in it where the guards passed food to the two detainees who had been assigned to be "class monitors." There were nine bunk beds in the cement room and a squat toilet at one end. There were two cameras, and near the one at the front of the room was a speaker and audio recording system. They did not turn the lights off at night.

When he arrived in the cell, the camp workers undid his handcuffs and told him that he was assigned to a top bunk. But

88   they told him that during the day he was not allowed to sit or lie on the bed. Instead he had to sit straight up. At this point in the interview, Adilbek demonstrated what this ramrod straight posture looked like, his chest out and his head held high. "Until they brought us stools, we had to sit on the bottom bunk just like this for hours at a time, staring at the wall or the TV that was on the wall. You could not move whenever you wanted. You had to get permission." As in Vera's camp thirty kilometers to the east, the detainees were forced by the automated surveillance system and the guards who monitored it to sit absolutely still for most hours of the day—a form of physical torment that prevented them from relaxing and over time began to wreak havoc on their bodies. "They sat between these beds on plastic stools, reciting the rules. You had to recite, whether you knew Chinese or not. And because the people had to sit there for such long hours, there were many people whose intestines 'fell down.'" Baimurat recalled, regarding the Qitai camp where many detainees suffered from rectal prolapses. "When they had such problems, they were finally allowed to see a doctor." Continuing, he described how detainees would be hooded, shackled, and escorted by police armed with automatic weapons to the hospital in a manner identical to Vera's experience.

Another former detainee named Payzilet who was held in the women's quarters of the same camps as Adilbek recalled that these digestive problems were complicated by the lack of hydration they received and the lack of nutrition and fiber in their rations. "Frequently it happened that we couldn't go to the toilet during our allotted time," she noted. "This is because we often only drank one or two bowls of thin soup and ate one or

two steamed buns without tea each day. It is hard to go to the
toilet quickly if you hardly drink anything."

Every former detainee I spoke with said that sleeping at
night was difficult. Adilbek recalled, "There were twenty-three
or twenty-four people in our cell, so some of us had to sleep
together in the bunk." They had to sleep head to feet on their
sides. As in Payzilet's and Vera's experience, they could not
cover their faces with their hand or the blanket to block out
the light. Not only were they watched by the cameras, but two
detainees were assigned to stand and guard them at night. "If
you spoke or moved, or if you failed to report others, you might
be taken out and beaten," Adilbek said.

For the first six months, the detainees did not leave the cell
except for weekly showers. "We just sat there and watched Xi
Jinping tours," Adilbek said. "We watched several hours on the
weekend, always about how prosperous China is." They were
not allowed to speak Kazakh or Uyghur. "We pretended to write
our characters and whispered to each other without moving our
mouths. Where are you from? What were you doing? Why are you
here? Some said they had gone to Kazakhstan, some were imams,
some had sold memory cards with religious teachings on them,
some said they had some religious content on their phones."

There was a loudspeaker on the wall. It would startle them
awake each morning. Within five minutes they had to get dressed
and make their beds "just as they do in the military." The guards
did not enter the cell to inspect this; they would just look through
the hole in the door or through the cameras. "They didn't come
into our room unless something was broken. If they came in,
they would yell at us to *baotou*." Jumping out of his chair, Adilbek

90   demonstrated what this looked like: hands clasped behind his neck, pulling his head down, while he squatted with the ease of someone who had been in this position of submission many times in his life.

Once per week they were allowed to take showers. Since they only had ten minutes for all twenty-three people to shower, and there were only five or six nozzles of cold water, they tried to prepare in their rooms as best they could. "We had to *baotou* until they opened the door and then we could run to the shower. We all rushed to do this, pulling on each other. It was impossible to get a shower if you didn't get there first. They gave us a towel, toothbrush, and some squares of soap that we had to fight over. There were always fights, but the guards would yell at us and so we always went quickly."

The detainees were pulled in different directions by the camp machine. In order to maintain a sense of dignity, they wanted to be clean. To survive, they wanted to have enough to eat. But because the camp made these things a scarce resource, they were forced to compete with each other. Often, though, the fear of the clubs and electric stunning devices of the guards, or beatings in the tiger chair, overwhelmed these desires. Over and over they were told and shown that they were animals and that their survival depended on the whims of the guards. "The guards had clubs and electric batons," Adilbek recalled. "If you went against them, they would beat you. I saw them hit us many times. It was common. When you didn't abide by the rule or if you talked back, they would beat us."

Adilbek said that sometimes the guards struck them hard, as if to punish them, but sometimes it was more like they were guiding them "like a farmer herding sheep." The *punishing blows*

came if they didn't speak "the national language," or Mandarin—
Adilbek used the name for the Chinese language that was used
in the camp. The *disciplining blows* came "if we stepped out of
line." A Han man who was briefly held with Uyghur detainees
in a detention center in the Southern city of Atush said, "The
police think that when they are hitting you that they are edu-
cating and changing you. They don't treat us as though we are
real human beings." These forms of physical abuse and training
resonate with Primo Levi's recollections from Auschwitz: "Some
of them beat us from pure bestiality and violence, but others beat
us when we are under a load almost lovingly, accompanying the
blows with exhortations, as cart-drivers do with willing horses."

Adilbek said that he and many of his fellow detainees tried
to follow the rules as best they could in order not to be hit. "But
sometimes when we were just walking, they would hit us. And
they always yelled at us when we were walking. They called us
livestock. Animals. They yelled, 'Move, move, move, you head of
a pig!'" The low-level guards were mostly Kazakhs and Uyghurs
who were watched by Han supervisors, but they all yelled at
the detainees in Chinese. Payzilet, the Kazakh detainee in the
women's quarters of Adilbek's camp, said that one particularly
cruel female Uyghur guard named Aygul would call Han male
guards to beat Uyghur female detainees that she recognized.
She remembered that Aygul would say, "I remember you used
to wear a veil, you deserve to be beaten." A Kazakh man named
Yerzhan Kurman said in a 2019 interview with the German
magazine *Die Zeit* that the Uyghur and Kazakh guards told the
detainees in his cell in a camp near the Kazakhstani border, "You
don't have the right to talk, because you are not humans. If you
were humans, you wouldn't be here."

It seemed clear to Adilbek that the way the guards treated them was systemic. The mechanisms of the camp reflected the mentality of the warden, who had almost unlimited power. "The ethnicity of the guards was not important," Adilbek said, shaking his head. "They had a head boss who made them act this way, and it was all being recorded on camera. When the bosses were coming, the guards would shout *baotou! baotou!* in the hall. The whole building would echo with this. The person in charge was a Han man with the surname Wang. It seemed like he came all the time. Some people would get so scared when he came that they would pee themselves. He came whenever he wanted."

Back at her camp in Ürümchi, Qelbinur said that the Han man whom Kadir reported to acted in similar ways. When Kadir received the order to expand their camp, he asked, "Are there going to be fifteen people in each cell?" He told Qelbinur that the Party official had laughed and told Kadir, "I am not asking you to build a hotel. I am asking you to build a camp. There should be fifty or sixty people in each cell."

Dehumanizing Muslims was something that the central leadership of the party-state had mandated at the beginning of the People's War on Terror. In 2014, Xi Jinping and other leaders described Uyghur terrorists and extremists as rats that needed to be chased and "beaten down" by everyone. A media campaign began to depict Uyghurs and Kazakhs deemed extremists as vermin and demons in wall-sized murals and state-media publications across the region. The establishment of an extralegal "smart" camp system to which all Muslims deemed "untrustworthy" could be banished routinized this demonization. This is why the Han neighbors of Qelbinur's student applauded when

a Uyghur man was led away—another rat had been caught in the
apartment building.

The Reeducation Sensorium

All of the former detainees I interviewed said that their world
began to revolve around immediate concerns: food, going to the
toilet, singing and reciting in Chinese. The outside world began
to fade. Yerzhan Kurman, a detainee who would later be forced
to work in a factory, said that during the first two months of
his detention in the camps, "I thought of my wife, Maynur, and
my three children." But he recalled that "sometime later, I only
thought about food." Like detainees held without formal sentences in other historical periods, time beat to the rhythm of
survival.

The sensorium of taste, smell, sound, and pain was brought
together in the rules that were posted on the walls of the cells.
"One of the rules in the camp was that detainees were not permitted to use the word *halal* or its Chinese equivalent, *qingzhen*,"
Adilbek remembered. "You just ate what was given to you. Each
time they would give a bowl. It wasn't even enough. They gave
us that and one or two steamed buns. Many people felt hunger
all the time. There was a slot at the bottom of the door where
they poured the food into a bowl."

The process of receiving this food was tied to singing patriotic songs or chanting prescriptive phrases, which was closely
watched over the camera and audio system. In Adilbek's case,
the "class monitors"—people like Vera who were assigned to
monitor the other detainees—were the ones who received the
food from the slot in the door after they all stood at attention

and sang as loudly as they could. As this was happening, the music would begin to play on the TV and they would sing the Chinese characters karaoke-style. "Sometimes they asked us to sing five or six songs before we ate," Adilbek said. "It is very difficult to sing like they wanted us to when you are hungry. Sometimes they would yell at us, 'Sing again! Sing again!' like it was a game for them. We didn't know which room was singing wrong. The whole camp, all of us in each cell, were singing as loudly as we could when the TV told us to sing."

In a separate interview, Payzilet, who was held across the camp in the women's section, confirmed this practice of singing for the thin vegetable soup that kept them alive. "Sometimes we had to sing dozens of times. Even if they were older people who didn't know the songs because they didn't know Chinese, they had to sing. They made them squat on their feet for two hours if they didn't fulfill their singing duty. I would be held responsible because I was the 'class monitor.' Sometimes the younger detainees would ask to be punished instead of them." At times, Payzilet was able to negotiate a lesser punishment for people who were sick or unable to squat. Demonstrating with hands held at shoulder level, she said, "They would make them stand facing the wall, with their two hands flat against the wall. If they let their hands fall, they would have to start over." All of this was watched over the cameras, assuring that detainees followed these bodily commands like contestants in a demented version of a reality TV show.

Even outside the camps, people understood that singing and chanting was connected to being fed inside the camps. Lu Yin, the Han woman who I interviewed in 2019, told me that, during a government visit to a Uyghur family, her hosts told her that, in the camps, "the guards ask, 'Who provides your daily food?' The answer is, 'Xi Jinping!' If you don't answer this way then you don't get fed!"

Several months into their detention, Payzilet and Adilbek began to have classes two or three times per week. As in most camps, there was a barrier that divided them from the teachers. "The chairs were chained to the desks so they could not move them," Adilbek recalled. "They were so close to the desks that the desks pressed into our stomachs."

In their camp in Wusu, their teachers were Kazakh, Mongol, Uyghur, and Han. They taught them elementary school–level characters and *pinyin*, even though some of the detainees had university degrees. They taught them more and more patriotic songs and made them memorize quotes from Xi Jinping. Those who did not know Chinese, like Adilbek, learned from the other students. "They told us, 'You are not here to learn things. It doesn't matter if you know things or not. You are being punished.'" So they did not care that other students wrote Adilbek's weekly "thought report" and that he did not have the ability to read it. "I think it said things like, 'I committed a crime. I'll never do that again. Now I'm learning seventy-five laws about extremism or fifteen sets of other laws.' I think it mentioned things like that, but I don't really know because the others helped me."

Over time, the daily violence of the routines enveloped the detainees. The long hours on stools, the rush to the showers, combined with the starvation diet, produced a dull numbness. On relatively rare occasions when the detainees were allowed out of their cells, Qelbinur and other camp workers noticed this transformation as well. Because the iron doors of the cells

96 were bound by a short chain, which allowed the door to open less than a foot, when the detainees were sent to the classrooms they had to duck down one at a time to exit. "The detainees had to crawl instead of walk when they were let out of the cell. When I saw them do this, the Han guards laughed at them, mocking them. The detainees had to crawl like dogs." The automatic way that the detainees did this action, silently, ducking one after another, trying not to draw attention to themselves, is what made them look like frightened animals.

She also noticed that in the cells where there was no plumbing, the guards often plugged their noses or wore face masks to block out the smell, like sanitation workers encountering filth. "When it was time to let them go to the class or shower, all the Han guards would wear masks," Qelbinur remembered. "When the door was open, a disgusting odor would permeate the entire floor. When I had a chance to look inside and see where the smell was coming from, I saw that they had a bucket located near the end of the beds. I imagined the way the others would watch someone when she used that bucket. They only let them clean the bucket once per week, so they had no choice but to use it. They had to live in that disgusting odor."

Qelbinur noted that, in other sections of the camp where they had toilets on each floor, the detainees were allowed to use them once per day. But they only had one minute, or they risked shocks from electric batons or blows from wooden clubs. The smell of excrement and sweat became the smell of fear and inhumanity. It affected the camp workers, even as detainees grew accustomed to it. In early 2018, a Han detention worker in a Uyghur majority county noted that the smell of the hundreds of detainees he helped to round up each day permeated the space, taking away his appetite.

Sometime in June 2017, Kadir asked Qelbinur to carry a big bag into the staff office of the camp. When she asked what was inside the bag, a coworker told her it was new underwear for the detainees. Since in that camp there were no showers, they had not been able to clean themselves for several months. "Their underwear was so dirty and smelled so bad, so Kadir wanted the guards to distribute underwear through the slot in the door when they handed out their steamed buns."

On another occasion, she saw the Han guards laughing in the courtyard next to a huge pile of detainee uniforms. Out in the open air, the smell was not as strong as they prepared to boil the uniforms. "I could see that there were lice everywhere. The guards were laughing. They told me, 'These lice were so tough.' It was simply a joke to them." The misery of thousands of detainees locked in their cells did not seem to matter.

Death in the Nursing Home

A number of months into their stay, Adilbek and Payzilet were transferred to a new camp, a converted nursing home on the northwest side of Wusu city. Before they were transferred, Adilbek said he had heard rumors that "it would be freer and the food would be better. But it wasn't like this."

In the nursing home camp cells, there were six bunk beds stacked three levels high like sleeper cars in a Chinese train. There were only 1.5 meters between the narrow bunks, and during the day detainees were not permitted to sit on the beds. There was a toilet and a shower in Adilbek's cell.

But almost immediately, Adilbek found that the discipline was harsher in his new surroundings. "I was the only Kazakh," Adilbek remembered. "The rest were Uyghurs. The guards were so rude to us. They beat people more often. They would kick us with their feet or hit us with a stick. After two days in the camp, the guards came in shouting, 'Hold your heads! Hold your heads! Hold your heads!' Luckily I was able to get down in front of others, so I was just kicked lightly. But others, even old men, were kicked harshly. They tried to kick people in the crotch on purpose with their boots. They wanted to hurt them. The next day, one of the old men could not stand."

Eventually it was discovered that Adilbek was not Uyghur and had been placed in the Uyghur cell by accident. "The guard asked, 'Why didn't you tell me you were Kazakh?' He slapped our 'class monitor' in the face. The guard took me to another room with a Tatar and seven other Kazakhs. After being transferred they didn't beat us anymore. But we could hear people screaming from the beatings in other rooms. They definitely mistreated the Uyghurs more than us."

Payzilet's new cell was less well equipped. "We just had a bucket to use for a toilet," she recalled. "There was a camera right above it, but gradually we got used to using it in front of each other and the camera. Sometimes the bucket overflowed and the guards would not let us take it out." Since Payzilet was assigned to be the "class monitor" for the cell, she tried to petition to empty it more often. "I told them, 'It is not hygienic. It will spread disease.'" But the guards just ignored her. Gradually they got used to living in the stench.

Sometime later, there was a major incident in the cell directly above Payzilet's. "In the middle of the night I heard a loud *thunk*." Almost immediately the lights went dark in the entire wing of the camp. Then Payzilet heard running. The next day, in whispers during their class period, she learned that the *thunk* was the sound of a Uyghur woman committing suicide. "She had jumped headfirst from the third-level bunk onto the floor," Payzilet told me. "She had a nine-year-old daughter and a one-year-old who had been taken to the orphanage, so she killed herself." Others in her cell said they wrapped her body in the blanket on her bunk and dragged it away. Soon after this, the officials built a clinic in the camp. She assumed that this was so that they could hide any other "abnormal deaths." Although Adilbek was held in another section of the camp, in a separate interview he confirmed the broad outlines of what Payzilet had heard. "I heard that someone killed themself too," he said.

Powerlessness

Inside the reeducation camps, it was difficult to maintain a sense of attachment to life and loved ones outside. Sometimes this detachment happened violently. Payzilet recalled that when she first arrived in the camp, young mothers who were detained with her were crying for their children. "Many of the young women were screaming because they had been forced to abandon their children in their homes. Then the police came and took them away. Several hours later, the women came back and were silent. They had been beaten severely." Through furtive whispers, she learned that some of them had left infants behind. "One told me that there was no one to take care of her baby because her husband had also been taken."

A Kazakh woman from a county near the border with China told me that when her sister, Nursulu Levai, and her husband

100   were taken, they left behind their children, who were sent to a different "camp," for kids. "Their children are growing up without their parents," she said with tears in her eyes. "Their oldest is six. When he and his brother are allowed to visit their grandparents once per week, they beg for their parents. At first they begged them in Kazakh, 'Please help us find our mom and dad!' Then they started to ask this in Chinese. They no longer say anything in Kazakh. Now most of the time they are just silent. They are so quiet." Chinese government documents show that in some Uyghur-majority areas, as many as 70 percent of children up through age five are now held in Mandarin-medium "Kindness Kindergartens" while their parents are in prisons, camps, or factories. Family separation is now endemic throughout Uyghur and Kazakh society.

Over time, the social isolation, family separation, and continuous surveillance became radically disempowering. For Adilbek, one of the most difficult experiences of life in the camp was being forced to misrepresent reality over and over again. This was particularly painful during monthly visits with his relatives in a visiting area adjacent to the camp. "When it was time to see a relative who came to see you, we were taken to the visiting area with a black hood over our heads and our hands shackled behind us," he said. "Before we entered the visiting area, the guards took our shackles and hoods off, and they also put their clubs down, so my relatives couldn't see this. There was always someone watching, taking notes. We had to say, 'Everything is good.' Before we went in, they said, 'Do not cry. Do not talk about your problems. You must say everything is great.'" Although everyone in the room knew that what Adilbek was forced to say was not true, no one was able to contradict this

staged reality. "There were cameras. They were watching everything. We couldn't say anything. I would just ask if my relatives could see my children, if they could contact them, and
they would shake their heads. They would not come alone. They
came with the village leader (*duizhang*). They were also very
scared." Remembering this later from the safety of Kazakhstan
brought tears to Adilbek's eyes. He wiped them away with the
back of his hand and drew in a long breath. "It is very difficult to
stay alive if you don't even have the right to speak, to say what is
happening to you."

Adilbek never understood why he had been taken. "When I managed to talk to the others, I realized all of them were innocent.
So I started to realize that we might not be released. I shouted
many times, asking why I had ended up here. I cried before them
many times. They told me they didn't know who took me there.
Or sometimes they said I must be aware of my guilt, since those
who had taken me there took me." There did not seem to be any
end or logic to the detention.

Camp time forced people to put their lives on hold indef-
initely. On a state-authorized visit to a camp in 2019, a North
American reporter furtively snapped an image of an Uyghur
inscription etched into the wall of a cell. It read, "This dorm
room is an outstanding dorm room. Hang in there my heart."
Many of the former detainees I interviewed said that one of the
most difficult aspects of being in the camp was not knowing
when, if ever, they might be released. The lack of control over
bodily movements, speech, hunger, and sickness wore their
bodies down physically and mentally. It made them distant from
their loved ones outside the camp. Time began to center around

102   staying alive by saying and doing what they were asked to do. Some of the former detainees I interviewed, such as Adilbek, said they did think of their children on a regular basis, but others said they lost track of important dates and in some cases they did not think of their family for long periods of time. The ritual time of birthdays, maternal and familial love, was overtaken by camp time. Everything fell away, except for the immediate demands of eating and drinking, using the toilet, staying healthy, and not stepping out of line.

This erasure of time recalls a haunting passage from Primo Levi regarding his own time in Auschwitz. "For months and years, the problem of the remote future has grown pale to them and has lost all intensity in the face of the far more urgent and concrete problems of the near future: how much one will eat today, if it will snow, if there will be coal to unload."

The Unfree

Erbaqyt Otarbai's nightmare began while he was unloading his truck in an ore yard near Ürümchi on August 18, 2017. The security guard told him that police from his hometown, Tacheng, six hours away near the border with Kazakhstan, were looking for him. The day before, they had interrogated him and confiscated his smartphone so they could examine it. Although he thought it was odd that they had traveled so far to meet him, they did not tell him he was being arrested. As a middle-aged Kazakh man who was not religious and had never been in trouble with the law, he was not really afraid. "I wasn't a criminal so I thought I had nothing to fear," he remembered. "The only thing I was worried about a bit since I was a truck driver was the possibility of some outstanding traffic tickets."

Hours later, though, when he was shackled in a "tiger chair" back in his hometown, a deep fear overwhelmed him. It has never left. "They told me to 'Sit here and answer our questions. Have you ever visited mosques, or prayed in Kazakhstan? Why did you go to Kazakhstan? Have you been in touch with Wahabi

104   Muslims? Do you drink alcohol?'" He told them that he did like
to drink and that he even used profanity at times, but he felt they
were not satisfied with his answers. "They said I had Facebook,
Instagram, and WhatsApp on my phone. 'Why were you using
these apps?' they asked." He replied that he had many friends in
Kazakhstan who used those apps, so he had downloaded them
to communicate with them before coming back to China to care
for his ailing father. The apps did not work in China anyway,
so he did not think they were a big deal. "Look for yourselves,
I haven't sent any illegal content." Then he remembered that,
though he really was not very devout, he had shared some religious videos before he knew that they were illegal.

  By this time it was the middle of the night. They took him
in shackles to a nearby hospital for a "health check" similar to
the one all Uyghurs and Kazakhs received: pictures of his face
from all sides, blood samples, and fingerprints. "They recorded
my voice and took an iris scan." Around 2:00 a.m., they took him
to the pre-trial detention center where he was shackled in heavy
manacles. As a way of welcoming him to the detention center, a
guard told him he was now in prison and smashed the top of his
head with a metal club. Blood streaming down his face, they led
him to a cell filled with other Muslim pre-criminals.

  In a repetition of the stories told in reeducation camp cells
across the region—from Qitai to Kashgar—the others in the
cell told him they had been taken because they had bought an
airline ticket to Turkey; a Kazakh was detained for studying
in Kazakhstan. Some were there because they had prayed too
often or stopped smoking. Others had given or taken cash loans
without getting government approval. Still others because they
had allowed someone else to use their ID to register a SIM card.

"When they heard that I was there for using WhatsApp, they told me that I would definitely be in the center for a long time." It turned out that, in this detention center, where the majority of the detainees were Kazakhs with ties to Kazakhstan, many had been detained because they had used WhatsApp.

Erbaqyt spent the next ninety-eight days in that detention center. Since it was a pre-trial jail, his treatment was even more brutal than the formal reeducation camps. "They woke us up at 6:00 a.m. and then made us run in the cell. It hurt because we had to wear heavy shackles. Sometimes our ankles bled," Erbaqyt recalled. "Then we were supposed to sit without moving on the edge of our shared platform. We were not allowed to move. Some of us would move eventually and then they would beat us."

Erbaqyt lived in fear of these beatings because they would cause suffering not just in the moment, but over days to come. "They hit us in the butt with wooden clubs that were around 1.5 meters long. The guards would make everyone else face the wall. Then the one who was being punished would lie facedown on the platform and two guards would beat him on the butt with the clubs. After you are beaten like this, it is almost impossible to sit, but the next day you have to sit again for many hours or you will be beaten again."

The brutality seeped into life in the cell and began to change them. There were fights between detainees. "I had a quarrel with others in the cell and then the guards beat me." Erbaqyt shuddered and drew silent, shaking his head as though trying to forget.

Eventually, Erbaqyt was transferred to a camp on the other side of Tacheng. As in Wusu, three hundred kilometers southeast, the new camp was a converted nursing home. With a police contractor on both sides, Erbaqyt and others in his cell were loaded into vans. "We were handcuffed, shackled, and hooded. The siren was blaring the whole way there."

As in all other camps, they were not allowed to sit on the bunk beds during the day. The lights were never turned off. They sat on stools and sang for their meals. They watched endless Chinese language political education lectures. Because of his working knowledge of Chinese, the classes, the singing, even the weekly "thought reports" were not too difficult for Erbaqyt. He was one of the lucky ones.

The Pet

It turned out that Erbaqyt knew some of the teachers. They had been his classmates or colleagues in their previous lives. One of them asked him to help keep the detainees in line. He said that they had to sit up straight and recite passionately in class, or else he could be punished. Erbaqyt remembered that he led the others in saying, "Thank you Uncle Xi" (*xiexie Xi dada*) as loudly as possible. He memorized twenty-two different patriotic songs.

At this point, Erbaqyt broke into a broad smile and his deep baritone filled the room as he broke into song. "Without the Chinese Communist Party, there would be no new China . . . ." He laughed at how absurd this sounded.

In November 2018, around a year after he arrived at the nursing home, the camp authorities asked if anyone wanted to work sewing clothes and doing other jobs. Several hundred people volunteered, but only 150 people passed the ideology and language tests necessary to begin this work. Again, Erbaqyt was one of these success stories.

The new factory was in the same compound as the camp, but in a different building. Inside the newly erected steel structure, they had set up around three hundred sewing machines. Two Han women were in charge of the detainees. They showed them how to sew parts of school uniforms, and then as they became more skilled, they began to make cloth napkins that had the logo for China Southern Airlines. At night, the detainees returned to their classroom in time to sing patriotic songs and study political thought. As he told me this, Erbaqyt broke into another song, a wide ironic smile on his face again. He snorted, and through his laughter said, "They never paid us. Otherwise," he joked, "I would have stayed."

A week or two into the new work regimen, the two Han factory wardens told the detainees that visitors were coming to see how they worked. "They made us repeat after them what we were supposed to say in Chinese: 'I was an unemployed person. I came here voluntarily to learn some skills. This is how the Party cares for us.'"

When the visitors came, he realized that they were journalists. He said he was near the back of the factory floor, so he did not even have a chance to recite the memorized lines. "They asked a few people who were at the front of the class questions." It appeared to him as though the journalists were satisfied with what they saw.

Near the beginning of 2019, Erbaqyt was unexpectedly released from the camp. His wife had become a Kazakh citizen and was petitioning for his return. For the next six months, he was held in the headquarters of the neighborhood watch unit near the location of his old apartment. "I could not go out. I

108   knew that if I went out without supervision I would be sent back to the camp. So instead, I cooked food for five administrators from the watch unit, I cleaned their offices and toilets, I boiled water for them to drink."

Two Han women in the Civil Affairs Ministry unit who were responsible for the detainees and former detainees from the neighborhood became his "life teachers." Every Monday he followed them to the neighborhood flag in front of the watch unit and participated in the flag raising. "I criticized myself loudly every time, saying that I didn't understand before how much the Party cared for me. And that I now cherish the Party. I sang the songs that I had learned in the camp."

He said that he kept a smile on his face all the time. He bowed and nodded whenever anyone approached him and he spoke only Chinese. "Inside I still felt like I was not a full person." Mimicking his reeducated smile, he said, "I just had to say, 'Okay, okay, good, good' (*xing, xing, hao, hao*) to everything they asked. I was like their pet."

"This is what reeducation taught me," he said with a big belly laugh.

Unfree Workers

Several months before Erbaqyt began working in the nursing home camp factory, Gulzira Aeulkhan was transferred from a camp in Ghulja, around six hundred kilometers south of Erbaqyt's camp. Gulzira, a thirty-nine-year-old mother of a toddler, had spent fifteen months of horrific abuse in crowded cells with up to sixty other detainees, most of whom were Uyghur. Detainees in her cell were shocked in the head with electric batons if they used the bathroom for longer than two minutes. Their closely

cropped hair masked some of the bruising. Detainees were given 109
dye to darken their hair and scalp before higher-level officials visited the camp. They were told to smile during the inspections.

Due to the relatively low level of her perceived "pre-criminal
offenses"—though according to documents supplied to the
UN by the Chinese government, all detainees in the camps had
not actually committed a crime—Gulzira had been placed in a
camp that had the least amount of security. What had marked
her as "untrustworthy" was a previous visit to Kazakhstan and
that she had watched Turkish TV shows in which women wore
hijabs. In her section of the camp, there was less of an emphasis
on ideological retraining. Instead, they studied Chinese all day,
every day. Kazakh and Uyghur languages were not permitted.

When she was released from the camp, Gulzira thought she
might be given greater freedom. But within several days, a local
village leader appeared with a document saying that she must
report for work at a glove factory. When she arrived at the plant,
she recognized her new boss, General Manager Wang Xinghua.
She had seen him several times back in the camp, on tours with
camp officials. She surmised that he must have picked her to
work in his factory while she was still in the camp.

Wang was contracted with Luye Shuozidao Trading Company, a manufacturer based in Baoding city, Hebei province.
Speaking in a state TV interview released in December 2018,
he said, "With the support of the government, we have already
recruited more than six hundred people." Two of these six hundred government "recruits" were Yerzhan Kurman, whose story
I began to tell in the previous chapter, and Gulzira.

In the interview, Wang went on to say that, since the
founding of the new factory in 2017, "We have generated

110   more than $6 million in sales. We plan to reach one thousand workers by the end of this year. We plan to provide jobs to fifteen hundred people by the end of 2019." In fact, the glove factory in Ghulja had now far surpassed the capacity of its parent factory, which back in Hebei employed fewer than two hundred employees. Moving manufacturing to Xinjiang made sense for the company, which sold 96 percent of its leather gloves across the border in Russia and Eastern Europe.

But there were other reasons why exponential growth was so easy. Since 2018, the state has provided subsidies to build factories and ship goods from Xinjiang. Construction of the factories was often funded by local governments in Eastern China as part of a "pairing assistance" program. Up to 4 percent of new factory's sales volume was subsidized in order to cover shipping expenses from the new location. Most important, there was a standing reserve of tens of thousands of desperate, traumatized detainees like Gulzira in nearby camps.

Since 2017, factories have flocked to Xinjiang to take advantage of the newly built industrial parks associated with the reeducation camp system and the cheap labor and subsidies that accompany them. In late 2018, the primary development ministry for the region, the Xinjiang Reform and Development Commission, circulated a statement that the camps or "vocational skills education and training centers" had become a "carrier" of economic stability. Because of this system, Xinjiang had attracted "significant investment and construction from coast-based Chinese companies." Since China sources more than 80 percent of its cotton from Xinjiang, there was a special emphasis placed on Chinese textile- and garment-related industries. In an effort motivated at least in part by rising labor costs among Han migrant workers on the east coast, by 2023 the state plans to move more than a million textile and garment industry jobs to the region. If they succeed, it will mean that as many as one in every eleven textile and garment industry jobs in China will be in Xinjiang. The 1,500 jobs at the glove factory in Ghulja are part of that number.

Broadly speaking, there are three primary tracks through which Uyghurs and other Turkic Muslims are involuntarily assigned to work in the newly built factories as part of the reeducation labor regime. First, many detainees in camps are placed in factories inside or adjacent to camps. Like Erbaqyt, they are assigned to work inside the same camp space in which they are held at night.

Second, some new industrial parks built in regional centers host a mix of former detainees, such as Gulzira, and "rural surplus laborers" who are not former detainees. These surplus laborers are chosen by government officials from self-employed populations of rural farmers and peri-urban Kazakhs and Uyghurs who previously found contingent work in heritage trades and service industries. Former detainees who join these surplus laborers in the urban industrial parks are often held in locked dormitories at night. Some "surplus laborers"—like migrants workers in Eastern China—are permitted to return to their own homes at night or to stay in freely chosen accommodations in the regional center.

Third, newly built county-level and smaller-scale "satellite factories" in rural areas host Uyghur workers near their homes. These worker populations of mainly women with young children are assigned by local village- and township-level authorities to work while their children are cared for in daycare facilities

112   while their husbands work in the city or are detained in camps.
While there are different levels of coercion in these tracks, all
three of them result in forms of family separation and dependence on the state and private industry proxies for training and
discipline in Chinese-speaking environments. Though they can
sometimes go home at night, like Muslim camp workers, they
are not permitted to quit their jobs without permission. All of
them are slotted into a spectrum of forced labor.

As documents used by state workers associated with the
camp system note, refusing "poverty alleviation" schemes, a
widely used euphemism for assigned factory work and other
forms of assigned labor, is regarded as a sign of untrustworthiness and religious extremism. The grassroots-level state
workers who partner with police stations and private and state-
owned enterprises to implement the campaign are charged with
providing employees from populations within their jurisdictions. They often accompany workers to the factories, and at
times act as intermediaries between factory management and
the workers. They also enforce discipline on the factory floor
and, in some cases, in dormitories. In a radical contravention
of the supposed "freedom" associated with market-based contract law, some state authorities appear to assume that the only
reason a Muslim worker may not want to be separated from
their families and work for low wages in a Han-managed factory is because of their aversion to contact with non-Muslims.
Forcing Uyghurs and Kazakhs to work in a Chinese-speaking
environment can then be framed by state workers and
employers as liberating them from their native way of life and
traditions. This framing elides the process of state and market

dependence that is created by dispossessing Uyghurs, Kazakhs, and Hui of their autonomy.

The glove factory where Yerzhan and Gulzira were sent appeared to have a mix of both former detainees and involuntarily assigned "surplus workers." Many arrived in the factory after briefly being released from the camp. Yet, according to a state report, it appears as though more than 1,800 others were sent to work in the industrial park in mid-2017, long before the first detainees were transferred from the camps. According to Yerzhan and Gulzira, these early arrivals were "track two" underemployed rural workers who were determined to be part of the "normal" population and assigned to work without first being placed in a camp.

Gulzira was told that, as a trainee, she was to be paid 600 yuan per month, approximately $100, one-third of the state-mandated minimum wage, for the first three months. She would also be paid a small amount, around 2 jiao (20 Chinese cents), per pair of gloves according to her "efficiency." She said, "The most skilled worker could sew sixty pairs a day. I tried my best, but I could only sew thirteen pairs." Since she did not have good eyesight, she found that it was impossible for her to improve her production levels. Speaking to reporter Ben Mauk, she said, "In the end, I worked there for a month and a half. It was piecework. I earned 1 jiao for every glove I finished. All told, I made more than two thousand gloves and earned 220 yuan. So, you see, it was like slavery."

Although there was less security in the factory, the detainees were not allowed to leave. In an interview with her in January 2020, months after she had fled across the Chinese

114   border to Kazakhstan, Gulzira told me there were checkpoints at
the entrance of the dormitory and factory where her ID and face
were scanned. She said, "We would have our bodies and phones
checked when we arrived and in the middle of the day. When we
were leaving for the dormitory at the end of the day, they would
check again because they were worried we might take a sewing
needle. After we got to know the police contractors, we asked
them, 'Why are you still here watching us?'" While they never
replied, she told me she knew that the answer to this question was that the security workers were monitoring whether
or not they were acting like submissive "reeducated" industrial workers. She noted that, like every other Turkic Muslim
she knew, her passport had been confiscated and that travel
beyond the parameters of their assigned locality—whether it
was an industrial park or the relative freedom of a village—was
not permitted. In addition, like the vast majority of assigned
workers, she had very little money with which to attempt to pay
someone to smuggle her out. Life at the factory was better than
life in the camp, but she understood that, in the new space, she
was being asked to prove that she had been truly reeducated and
had become an industrial worker.

Outside of the discipline of the factory and industrial park,
the infrastructure of material walls continued to be a part of
her life. Every night after work she and other detainees were
taken by buses to a makeshift dormitory around three kilometers away. In the dormitory, detainees were permitted to walk
around the compound, but they were not permitted to leave the
premises. According to reporting from the *Globe and Mail*, the
workers "received readings in the factory before work and, at

day's end, forty-five-minute Chinese lessons in the dormitory, where they were watched at night by an official."

Both Yerzhan and Gulzira were permitted to visit their families for several hours during one day on the weekend. A company bus would ferry them back and forth from the dormitory to their home villages. A month into their "training," however, they found out that these trips were quite costly. Bosses at the factory, such as General Manager Wang, told them that, because of the expense of the shuttle service and their food, their 600 yuan salary would be slashed in half. Yerzhan later recalled, "I worked on a production line for fifty-three days, earning 300 yuan in total."

Government documents show that, in Kashgar Prefecture in 2018, 100,000 detainees were scheduled to move to work in newly built industrial parks and satellite factories. In a county between Wusu, where Adilbek the sheep farmer was held, and Kuitun, where Vera, the University of Washington student, was held, 15,600 "surplus laborers," drawn from a population of around 45,000 total Muslims, were put to work through such labor schemes. Other prefectures are aiming for similar numbers. In Kashgar, for each detainee that was put to work, the factory owners would receive 5,000 yuan dispersed over three years. These subsidies were likely put in place to prevent the type of wage garnishment that Yerzhan and Gulzira experienced. However, since the factories function as an extension of the camp system, operating in a legal gray zone outside of civil and human rights, prevention of worker abuse falls on the moral codes of people like General Manager Wang. As an industrialist acting as a proxy for the reeducational state, he knew just as well

116   as Yerzhan or Gulzira that any complaint, any slowdown in production, could result in their replacement with other detainees.
He could treat them in any way he wanted.

Newly built industrial parks in Northwest China occupy
a threshold between reeducation camps and private industry,
proletarianization and forced labor. State documents note over
and over again that the new industrial parks are being built to
instill undefined "life skills" in Uyghur and Kazakh detainees
and other Muslim surplus laborers. What is often left unsaid in
state-approved documents is the way these factory spaces function as an archipelago of near total institutions at the periphery of
the Chinese social contract—an implicit agreement that a state
will protect its citizens in exchange for their loyalty. For Uyghurs,
Kazakhs, and Hui citizens from Xinjiang, this social contract has
been shattered as the prison archipelago is turned toward a mode
of colonial-capitalist production—a reeducation labor regime—
that eats into the vitality of their social reproduction. The documents of the workers in Xinjiang internment factories are
confiscated or their IDs are marked as non-passing, placing them
under a universalized form of unfreedom. These types of coerced
labor are subsidized and directed by the state and operationalized
by a complex web of surveillance practices and a logistics system
that is bringing the Chinese factory to the Uyghur and Kazakh
homelands. All of this material development is authorized by the
threatening presence of hundreds of internment camps, which
signify the power of the state over Muslim life.

Importantly, the effects of this system are not limited to
Northwest China, or even to China itself. Nearly all the gloves
that are made by detainees in the satellite factory of the Luye
Shuozidao Trading Company are sold abroad. On the company's

Alibaba distribution site, they note that the price of their gloves ranges from between $1.50 and $24.00 per pair depending on the style of the glove and quantity purchased. Some are distributed by the upscale Hong Kong—based boutique Bread n Butter, which has outlets in malls around the world where they likely are sold for far more. In any case, the price at which these gloves are sold is exponentially higher than the price workers are paid per pair. This system of expropriation—a type of state-authorized theft—is justified by the rhetoric of "poverty alleviation," of "aiding Xinjiang" with the gift of the cultural capital of Chinese language knowledge. Or it's framed as Han factory owners helping the detainees to achieve the "life skills" of disciplined industrial interns.

In an essay written in adulation of the internment factory complex, a Ghulja county official wrote that, when the Turkic Muslim farmers and herders arrived at the factory, they "took off their grass shoes, put on leather shoes, and became industrial workers." The counterfactual imagery of "backward" minority people who wore primitive "grass" shoes, being given the gift of factory discipline through internment, precisely captures the spirit of the skills training process from the perspective of state workers and contractors. Over and over in a regional state media video valorizing the implementation of coercive job programs, the reporter noted that the Muslim workers did not even pause to look up at the camera during the filming. The reporter interpreted this as a sign of their excellent work ethic as newly trained "high quality" workers. Both Yerzhan and Gulzira mentioned that their managers emphasized that the gloves they were making were for export, so the quality of their sewing had to be very high. The training they received in "human quality" had to be reflected in the quality of the gloves they mass-produced.

The introduction of state-directed, Han-exclusive corporate power over Uyghur and Kazakh life has the effect of accelerating the alienating effects of factory labor across ethnic and class differences. Alienation, removing the individual from the ownership of their labor as workers and, in this case, from their autonomy as Turkic Muslim individuals, is in fact a primary feature of the reeducation factory. By turning a population of people regarded as not deserving of legal protections into a permanent underclass, state authorities and private industrialists hope that they will extend the market expansion of the Chinese textile and garment industry. They are building a colonial frontier in capitalist accumulation. This system of controlled labor is "carried" forward by a massive reeducation system, a mechanism of infrastructural state power that ensures that this class of interned laborers cannot rise up as a class for themselves. In fact, because of this extralegal system, the only thing that protects Turkic Muslim workers from expropriation and violence is the goodwill of their Han managers. As indicated by the payment scheme at the glove factory, worker protections often appear to center on management "investment" in the quality of Turkic workers even while worker well-being and social relationships are viewed as valueless.

The Survivors

Since the factories function as an extension of the camp system, outside the rule of law and at the margin of the social contract, factory managers can treat Uyghur, Kazakh, and Hui workers as though they are disposable. In December 2018, managers threatened Gulzira in order to get her to sign a one-year work contract. They told her that if she did not sign, she would be sent back to the camp. There is a nearly limitless standing reserve of other detainees. In the race to the bottom—the least cost for the most productivity—the reeducation factory in Ghulja is at the limit of contemporary global capitalism.

The unfreedom Gulzira, Yerzhan, and Erbaqyt experienced is connected to slavery in general, but it is also specific in the way it is manifested on the factory floor, or in the cases of Vera, Qelbinur, and Baimurat, in forced labor as English tutors, Chinese teachers, or data police. Their stories point out that ethnoracialized forms of slavery, even when it is manifested as forms of unfree (but paid) labor, is still a reproduction of a relationship of domination. Looking back at his time in the camp and factory from the relative safety of Kazakhstan, Erbaqyt recalled, "It took me two or three months to come to myself. But even now I don't feel completely safe. I will never feel free ever again." Life had taken on a new seriousness. As a survivor, he, and many of the other detainees I interviewed, felt they had lost something of their humanity—they felt themselves pushed toward asociality and cruelty.

"We often became hopeless. Sometimes we really felt hatred toward the Chinese people, to the point where I would catch myself thinking that I could kill Chinese government workers just to feel something," Erbaqyt said with a sad smile. "But then I think about all the Han Chinese people I've met who also criticize Xi Jinping, who curse him. So I can't blame the Chinese people for this; they are victims too."

Erbaqyt did not want to believe that humans were intrin-
sically brutal and self-centered, and that when assisted by the
power of reeducation technologies—from cameras to camps—
they would become people without inhibitions. He felt that,
when confronted with such extreme powers over life, social
mores and empathy are often worn down and silenced. In her
work as a camp instructor, Qelbinur saw this in action. She
heard her Han colleague exclaim, "Isn't this the twenty-first
century? How can this be happening now?" Initially she sobbed
when she saw elderly Uyghurs presented to her in chains as
her "students." But over time, she stopped crying so often. It
became easier to join the swarms of functionaries in the system.
Despite her role in the system, most of her fellow Muslims recognized her actions for what they were: a strategy of surviving
the machine of reeducation. Given the opportunity, it appeared
that Erbaqyt would join Primo Levi in freely absolving "anyone
whose complicity in the crime was minimal and whose coercion
was maximal."

Erbaqyt is nostalgic, in the true sense of the term—a deep
painful longing—for his former life. "Sometimes I feel content
with the fact that I'm back [in Kazakhstan] and I'm reunited
with my family. And I think, 'This is enough.'" Yet, though he
felt this way at times, in waking dreams, his chest heaving,
he would think about an image seared in his mind of the lines
of Kazakh and Uyghur women he saw with their hair cropped
short, the blankness in their eyes as they shuffled by, denuded
and unfree. "We have our own customs. Kazakh women always
wear a headscarf to protect their dignity. They made them take
this off, then they made them cut off their beautiful hair. There
they were with their white hair, exposed."

For Erbaqyt, the survivors were people who had isolated themselves from feeling anything. They betrayed each
other and themselves in an effort to survive. In the nursing
home camp in Wusu, Payzilet recalled hearing countless other
detainees openly denounce others from their communities who
had not yet been detained. "They said, 'Why did you take me and
not this other person? They were more religious than me,'" she
recalled. "This is why the camps became so crowded. Everyone
was denouncing each other in order to save themselves. I became
a 'class monitor' for the same reason."

The survivors sang and smiled when they were asked. But
they lost something through the process. Some lost their sanity,
but others simply became cold and blank. They entered what
Primo Levi refers to as the "gray zone": the domain of the data
police, two faced camp workers, the cell monitors, the infor-
mants, or even more often, the sweepers, cooks, and seamsters.
They became the survivors who build, maintain, and feed the
machine of reeducation that has eaten so deeply into Uyghur,
Kazakh, and Hui society.

Unlike previous internment camp systems, the Xinjiang
reeducation camps employ pernicious technologies, which
bring the totalizing power relations of the camps outside into
factories and communities. They bring a ferocious and desperate loneliness into everyday life, tearing apart communities, turning children against their parents. It is the engineers
of these systems—the algorithm tinkerers, the face recognition designers, the DNA mappers, the "smart" pedagogists—
for whom Erbaqyt and the others reserve their more precise
and subtle judgment of blame for the crime that has been committed against their humanity. Like the camp commanders and

122   factory managers who enforce the cruelty of the system, they are guilty of the complex and passionate work of unthinking their humanity. As much as they might claim the Eichmann defense that they were "just doing their jobs" and no one around them told them they were doing something wrong, they were in fact purposefully designing systems of control and automating forms of racialization.

It is their inhumanity that Erbaqyt feels reflected in the flashes of hatred he now feels when his sad smile freezes. Life in the camps has taught him to close himself off, encased in incomprehensible feelings, forever the hunted of the world.

Behind Seattle Stands Xinjiang

In 2016, Sun Jian decided to leave Seattle and return home. After thirteen years at Microsoft, Sun, the principal research manager of Microsoft Research Asia, decided to join an exciting computer vision startup called Megvii. Like Vera Zhou, the University of Washington student, who would fly home for a long weekend with her boyfriend around a year later, he went to SeaTac Airport and boarded a plane for the People's Republic.

The company Sun joined, Megvii—or "Mega Vision"—was founded by a pair of graduates from Tsinghua University. In 2016, it was in the midst of a rapid expansion in the Internet of Things (IoT) market in China. A year before, they—along with many other computer vision startups based in China—had received a massive MegaFace face recognition dataset from the Paul G. Allen School of Computer Science and Engineering at the University of Washington. It was sets like this that they used to train their core software program, or algorithm, Face++ to detect patterns—similarities and differences—in faces. Over this time, they shifted away from building automated tools for

124 ecommerce that compared millions of digital images to each other, toward facial recognition applications. By the end of 2017, they had developed "in-depth partnerships" with police departments in twenty-six cities and regions across China, including the Uyghur region—Xinjiang. This data-intensive, public-facing work, along with partnerships with the Ministry of State Security, and the Counter-Terrorism Leading Group, China's version of Homeland Security, helped them to rapidly build their capacities. By moving into this domain, they were able to train the Face++ algorithm with the Ministry of State Security database of state-issued IDs for nearly 1.4 billion Chinese citizens, including the high-resolution scans of Xinjiang faces that were drawn from each Muslim citizen in 2017.

Over the years, Megvii had built deep connections with Microsoft and Vera's school, UW. First in 2012, former Microsoft vice president Kai-Fu Lee used his own venture capital firm, Sinovation, to provide startup funds to the company. Then in 2014, Lee helped to broker an investment deal between Megvii and China's largest technology company, Alibaba. This partnership gave them access to the images on Alibaba's Taobao ecommerce platform, a relationship that they would later deny. Megvii also began to poach other Microsoft employees, or recruit from its pipeline, the UW Computer Science and Engineering School.

In 2017, Jue Wang, a recent PhD from UW and a lead designer for the Seattle-based software company Adobe also joined the startup. A principal scientist at the company who had built a number of the features of the latest iteration of Photoshop, Jue took up a position leading a new division of the company, Megvii Research USA, located less than a mile from Microsoft headquarters. He and more than a dozen other young computer scientists started the Megvii branch in the Redmond office, a nondescript beige two-story building surrounded by towering Douglas firs. The office was like any other Silicon Valley tech startup: They were simply coders and designers doing the intricate work of making objects in images searchable by breaking them down into smaller and smaller parts, solving the problem of doing it faster and faster. There was nothing sinister about the Megvii office, or the people that worked there. They weren't secretly trying to undermine American values or threaten the future of human autonomy. Reading through work environment assessments of former employees, it is clear that like most tech workers they thought they were making the world a better place. Their primary complaint was the lack of fruit in the break room. It was all perfectly banal.

As writer and tech worker Xiaowei Wang noted about their observations of Megvii's Beijing work culture: "It didn't just remind me of Silicon Valley. It *was* Silicon Valley." Megvii Research USA was surrounded by the titans of the world of technology—Microsoft, Amazon, Adobe. It was six miles away from one of the world's wealthiest neighborhoods—Medina, Washington, home to Bill Gates, Jeff Bezos, and other global elites. In many ways the Xinjiang reeducation tools were a product of this world. Microsoft Research Asia, the incubator that gave rise to Megvii, was itself widely known to be the "cradle of Chinese artificial intelligence." After the *Intercept* obtained a 52 gigabyte dataset of internal police documents from Xinjiang that was built using Oracle software, the executive vice president of Oracle, Ken Glueck, noted that nearly all major US tech firms—including IBM, Amazon, and Google—have been entangled in Chinese surveillance technology development.

Megvii was on its way to becoming a global player. What set Megvii apart was that, by 2017, Face++ was poised to be one of the first applications of deep learning systems to be implemented in the real-life situations of hundreds of millions of people. Like its primary rivals—the facial recognition startups Yitu and Sensetime—it was around 2017 that Megvii received large injections of state capital to build data-intensive "smart" security projects of localities across the nation. While Yitu provided its code to the leading camera maker Dahua and Sensetime partnered with Dahua's rival, the state contractor HikVision, Megvii took a different path. First it collaborated with Alibaba to provide identity security in their Taobao and Alipay platforms—the Chinese equivalents of Amazon and PayPal, respectively. It also began a partnership with Chinese smartphone manufacturer Vivo, to build their flagship X21 phone, which rivaled the iPhone X's face recognition security system. Rather than partnering directly with a state-owned camera maker, Megvii hired a director of the military contractor China Electronics Technology Group Corporations, HikVision's parent company, and developed their own camera line, allowing them to go into the "counter-terrorism" business on their own. As an employee of the company remarked in an online forum in 2019, the people at the company were "really smart." They demonstrated that "public security makes profit."

Yet, despite the ethical implications of moving into state security for one of the world's leading authoritarian states, when Sun took the plunge and joined the China-based tech startup financed by his former partner, he noted that, in many ways, it felt as though the culture of the new company was nearly identical to that of Microsoft; it was just that "everyone seemed to be ten years younger." Like many other tech firms, the company—headquartered in a glassy Beijing office building that looked like any other Silicon Valley startup—was doing basic computer science, building algorithms to aid computers in reading faces, people, objects, texts, scenes, behaviors, and images for a wide range of applications. Sun's motto was, "There are no bad algorithms, only bad data."

Yet, despite, or perhaps because of, the "no bad algorithm" ethos that pervaded the company, and most computer vision firms, the applications Megvii was working on were having profound effects in Chinese counter-terrorism operations far from the beige office building in Redmond or the white-walled showrooms in Beijing.

The Terrorism Discourse

The face-scan machine at the hotel check-in desk in Ürümchi was a white machine about a foot wide and a foot and a half tall with rounded corners in the style of Apple products. Above the HD screen were two LED lights that shone on the person staring into the screen. Below the screen was a flat scanner where the person was to place their ID. In the lower left corner, a rainbow-colored Megvii logo announced the branding of the algorithm that linked the face peering into the screen to the Xinjiang policing system. The software behind that logo—programmed code built from Seattle to Ürümchi—is what gave the machine the ability to verify the identity of the face to the image on an ID and compare it to thousands upon thousands of blacklisted faces in less than a second.

Speaking in Uyghur, I asked the clerk behind the desk if I should use the machine to verify my ID. A bit incredulous, he

128   responded, "Are you Uyghur?" I laughed and waved my passport at him and said, "No, I'm a foreigner, but I've lived here for a long time." He smiled, and said, "This machine isn't for you. It is just for local people. I'll have to scan your documents manually." Since I had last visited the Uyghur region in June 2015, a lot had changed. By April 2018, there were checkpoints at most jurisdictional boundaries and face-scan machines at the entrances to every residential area. Around forty of my Uyghur friends, former students, and colleagues had disappeared into the camp system. I ran into a few of those who had not yet been taken on the streets, and in quick conversations they confirmed that our mutual friends were gone. The "People's War on Terror" that the Megvii system supported had made nearly all Muslims in the region detainable.

To understand what counter-terrorism means in the Chinese context, it is necessary to take a step back two decades to October 11, 2001. It was on the one-month anniversary of the September 11 attacks that Chinese officials first used the term "East Turkestan terrorist" to describe Uyghur protestors and suicide attackers. Three months later, in January 2002, the State Council Information Office of China issued a public report that revised the past history of Uyghur civil protest and political violence—changing the already problematic term ethnic "separatist," since most Uyghur protests were directed toward local injustices rather than national self-determination—to the dehumanizing label "terrorist." In August 2002, Chinese authorities guided a Beijing-based FBI investigation of Uyghur "terrorism" in China. Facing mounting pressure to build a global coalition to back invasions of Afghanistan and Iraq, the Bush administration added the phantom, Pakistan-based East Turkestan Islamic

Party to a global terror list, the United Nations following suit soon after. A little over a year later, in December 2003, China's Ministry of State Security, Megvii's future partner, released a list of "terrorist organizations" and individuals—all of them Uyghur. Over the next two decades, like Muslims everywhere, the Uyghurs were "terrified," meaning their embodied appearance, religious practice, and political actions were turned into the object of the terrorism discourse. This produced what the scholar David Brophy refers to as a racialized "bad Muslim" slot that opened up a state of exception in civil and human rights— allowing Uyghurs as a whole to be treated as undeserving of basic protections. In China, terrorism came to mean any activity by ethnoracial others that is perceived as resisting the sovereignty of the state, regardless of the harms caused by that perceived threat.

It was in the period post-2014, as Megvii was hitting its stride, that Alibaba (Megvii's primary investor) began to work with the Ministry of State Security in counter-terrorism operations, which in the context of China means Uyghur and Kazakh surveillance. Megvii took on a key role in that operation, particularly outside of Xinjiang. According to numerous reports, Megvii was also made an official technical support unit of the Xinjiang Public Safety Video Laboratory. A report published by the Chinese state media company Xinhua in December 2017 stated that, through its work in public security and counter-terrorism, "thousands of illegal fugitives were arrested in key areas such as the three stations and one zone (bus stations, train stations, subway stations, and airports), public squares, parks, and border inspection zones; and [their] actual combat effectiveness received high recognition from the

130   Information Bureau of the Ministry of Public Security, the Ministry of State Security, and the Anti-Terrorism Leading Group." In keeping with Sun's "no bad algorithm" ethos, Megvii vice president Xie Yinan told National Public Radio, "We just provide the government the technology, and they do their job with it." In a conversation with investigative journalist Kai Strittmatter, Xie confirmed that Chinese state security services were some of their largest customers and that police from across the country were using their cameras. Xie said, "Our algorithm can support networks of 50,000 to 100,000 surveillance cameras. We can tell you what kind of person you'll find in a given place at a given time. We can ask, 'Who is that? Where is he? How long is he there for? Where's he going now?'" He noted that, "Through facial recognition, we perceive information such as your identity, your age, your gender, your ethnicity."

When Vera Zhou left the University of Washington for Xinjiang in 2017, communities within less than fifty miles of her home had already operationalized Safe City systems explicitly designed to be supported by the Face++ algorithm. It may have been the Face++ system that was responsible for why the police stopped her as she walked past a camera when she went shopping outside the grid of her neighborhood watch unit. Industry assessments of Face++ applications said that it was being used in "smart camps" and "mosque surveillance"—allegations that Megvii spokespeople later claimed were not true.

On October 7, 2019, bolstered by widespread bipartisan support and overwhelming evidence of human rights harms caused by technological surveillance, the US government placed eight Chinese technology firms on a list that blocks US citizens from selling goods and services to them. The listing noted that

Megvii, along with Yitu, Sensetime, Hikvision, and Dahua, were placed on this list because they were "acting contrary to the foreign policy interests" of the United States.

The listing hit Megvii hard. In March 2019, they had prepared to take the company public on the Hong Kong Stock Exchange. They had hired a world-class public relations firm called Brunswick Group to aid in the process of building investor interest in the English-speaking world. As news broke that Megvii was deeply involved in Chinese counter-terrorism, Brunswick director Matt Miller, a former business reporter for Bloomberg, began an aggressive damage control effort. He assigned a Hong Kong—based partner at the firm, Ginny Wilmerding, to contact organizations ranging from Human Rights Watch to the Australia Strategic Policy Institute to request that they downplay Megvii's involvement in Chinese policing and Xinjiang human rights abuse.

When I published a report that implicated Megvii in Chinese counter-terrorism for the Center for Global Policy, Miller and Wilmerding contacted me as well. They said that, in 2018, Megvii made less than $2 million in Xinjiang (approximately 1 percent of their revenue for that year), and that they did not make any revenue in Xinjiang during the first six months of 2019. They downplayed the dozens of reports that Megvii's algorithms would become a central component of China's counter-terrorism as "conflation" made by third-party marketers. Speaking on behalf of Megvii, Wilmerding stated that the company had not developed "any solutions targeting specific ethnic groups." Yet, before the effects of Chinese counter-terrorism were widely known to the world, at the end of 2017, the director of the Megvii's security vision said that, in a single Chinese city, over just 47 days of counter-terrorism operations, "76 fugitives had been captured, during which 9.5 million faces had been collected, 378 million faces had been compared, 278 early warnings issued, and 274 people had been intercepted at a rate of 98.9 percent." Like many other facial recognition companies in China, Megvii developed a "Uyghur alarm" tool that attempted to automate the detection of Uyghurs based on the ethnoracial phenotypes of their faces as they passed in front of video cameras. These are the ethnoracialized Muslim lives that Brunswick Group and the engineers in Megvii's Beijing and Seattle offices decided did not deserve protections from their technologies.

COVID Technologies of Forgetting
The COVID-19 pandemic carried with it many other instances of forgetting. In April 2020, Amazon, the world's wealthiest technology company, received a shipment of 1,500 heat-mapping camera systems from Megvii's rival Chinese surveillance company Dahua. Many of these systems, which are worth approximately $10 million, were to be installed in Amazon warehouses to monitor the heat signatures of employees and alert managers if workers exhibited COVID-19-like symptoms. Other cameras included in the shipment were distributed to IBM and Chrysler, among other buyers.

As the COVID-19 pandemic began to move beyond the borders of China in early 2020, a group of medical research companies owned by the Beijing Genomics Institute or BGI—another entity whose Xinjiang subsidiaries have been placed on the US no-trade list—has radically expanded, establishing 58 labs in 18 countries and selling 35 million COVID-19 tests to more than

180 countries. In March 2020, companies such as Russell Stover's Chocolates and US Engineering, a Kansas City–based mechanical contracting company, bought $1.2 million worth of tests and set up BGI lab equipment in University of Kansas Medical System facilities.

Megvii also capitalized on the pandemic. They deployed heat-mapping systems to hospitals, supermarkets, campuses in China, and in airports in South Korea and the United Arab Emirates.

Yet, while the speed and intention of this response to protect workers in the absence of an effective national-level US response was admirable, these Chinese companies are also tied up in forms of egregious human rights abuses. As Sanjana Varghese has noted recently, the "humanitarian experimentation" work of companies like BGI and Dahua in countering COVID-19 also doubles as technologies of population management. And it masks their involvement in the system of dehumanization that has placed as many as 1.5 million Muslims in internment camps.

Setting aside Amazon's own role in involuntary surveillance that disproportionately harms ethno-racial minorities, the company's purchase of Dahua heat-mapping cameras recalls an older moment in the spread of global capitalism that was captured by historian Jason Moore's memorable turn-of-phrase: "behind Manchester stands Mississippi." What Moore meant by this, in his rereading of Fredrich Engels's analysis of the textile industry that made Manchester, England, so profitable, is that many aspects of the British Industrial Revolution would not have been possible without the cheap cotton produced by slave labor in the United States. In a similar way, the ability of Seattle, Kansas City, and Seoul to respond as rapidly as they have

134   to the pandemic relies in part on the way systems of oppression in Northwest China have opened up a space to train biometric surveillance algorithms. The protections of others depend on forgetting about college students like Vera Zhou or farmers like Adilbek. It means ignoring the dehumanization of thousands upon thousands of detainees and unfree workers.

At the same time, Seattle also stands before Xinjiang. Chinese state funding, global terrorism discourse, and US industry training are three of the primary reasons why a Chinese fleet of companies now lead the world in face and voice recognition. This process was accelerated by a war on terror that centered on placing Uyghurs, Kazakhs, and Hui within a complex digital and material enclosure, but it now extends throughout the Chinese technology industry where data-intensive infrastructure systems produce flexible digital enclosures throughout the nation, though not at the same scale as in Xinjiang.

China's vast and rapid response to the pandemic has further accelerated this process by rapidly implementing these systems and making clear that *they work*. Because they extend state power in such sweeping and intimate ways, they can effectively alter human behavior. But the Chinese approach to the pandemic is not the only way to stop it. Democratic states like New Zealand and Canada, which have provided testing, masks, and economic assistance to those forced to stay home, have also been effective. These nations make clear that involuntary surveillance is not the only way to protect the well-being of the majority, even at the level of the nation.

In fact, numerous studies have shown that surveillance systems support systemic racism and dehumanization by making targeted populations detainable. The past and current US administrations' use of the Entities List to halt trade with companies like Megvii, while important, is also producing a double standard, punishing Chinese firms for automating racialization while funding American companies to do similar things. Increasing numbers of US-based companies are attempting to develop their own algorithms to detect racial phenotypes, though through a consumerist approach that is premised on consent. By making automated racialization a form of convenience in marketing things like lipstick, companies like Revlon are hardening the technical scripts that are available to individuals. As a result, in many ways race continues to be an unthought part of how people interact with the world. Police in the United States and in China think about automated assessment technologies as tools they have to detect potential criminals or terrorists. The algorithms make it appear normal that black men or Uyghurs are disproportionately detected by these systems. They stop the police, and those they protect, from recognizing that surveillance is always about controlling and disciplining people that do not fit into the vision of those in power. The world, not China alone, has a problem with surveillance.

To counteract the increasing banality, the everydayness, of automated racialization, the harms of biometric surveillance around the world must first be made apparent. The lives of the detainable must be made visible at the edge of power over life. Then the role of world-class engineers, investors, and public relations firms in the unthinking of human experience, in designing for human reeducation, must be made clear. The webs of interconnection—the way Xinjiang stands behind Seattle—must be made thinkable.

This book emerged out of the bravery of storytellers. I would like to first thank the courageous Uyghurs, Kazakhs, Hui, and Han people who risked so much to tell me their stories. Vera Zhou and Caiyun Ma welcomed me into their lives, telling deeply intimate, painful stories of how their lives had been torn apart. A community in Kazakhstan did the same, spending many hours waiting to speak with me, talking through their tears, baring their souls. As COVID swept around the globe, Uyghurs in locations under lockdown shared their Skype screens with me, pouring their hearts out to a stranger on the other side of the world. I hope that this book is a small form of compensation for all of their emotional labor. And I hope it aids in their slow recovery from the trauma that never seems to end.

Many of these conversations happened only because of the commitment and fearlessness of a research assistant in Kazakhstan, who must remain nameless, and here in Seattle a resolute assistant named Akida Pulat. Akida herself lost her mother, my colleague Rahile Dawut, to the reeducation camps in 2017. Her courage in listening to stories along with me from inside the camps—confronting the horror of it all head-on—was monumental. Akida, you inspire us all.

I also want to thank the colleagues and friends who pushed and prodded me to write *In the Camps*. Laura Murphy, Rian Thum, and Jeff Wasserstrom—this book would not have happened without you. Along the way Gene Bunin and Serikzhan Bilash provided logistical support. At *SupChina* Anthony Tao gave me space to explore Han and Uyghur perspectives on the effects of digital enclosure. At *ChinaFile* Susie Jakes, Jessica Batke, and Sara Segal-Williams provided me with Chinese state documents and critical feedback on early versions of sections that appear in this book. At *Noema* Rosa O'Hara and Peter Mellgard offered me a platform to develop some of the book's ideas. At the *Guardian* Amana Fontanella-Khan and Oliver Conroy helped me think through some ideas that found a place in the final chapter. Troves of internal police documents provided to me by the *Intercept* as well as hours and hours of conversation with Yael Brauer shaped the conceptual and analytic framing of the book. Conversations with my academic mentors and colleagues Sareeta Amrute, Sasha Su-Ling Welland, and Carolina Sanchez Boe likewise strengthened my approach to the project.

At Columbia Global Reports the patient and thorough guidance, reading, and support of Jimmy So and Nicholas Lemann has significantly strengthened the book. Their advice on organization and evocative detail has made the story come alive in new ways. Camille McDuffie's passion for the project has made it a joy to work with the press. Together they have helped me move between the worlds of social science and literary nonfiction. I am deeply in their debt.

Finally, my partner, Jennifer Byler, has always been my first and best reader. Her belief in this book has pushed me to try my utmost to make it a story that strains to represent the immense suffering that confronts our friends in Northwest China. Ultimately, this book is dedicated to our friends A.A., E., Rahile Dawut, D.M., A.S., Perhat Tursun, and Y., who disappeared into the camps in 2017 and 2018. Not a day goes by that we do not think of you.

My book *Terror Capitalism: Uyghur Dispossession and Masculinity in a Chinese City* (Duke University Press, 2021) examines the economic drivers that led the camp system. Drawing on ethnographic fieldwork conducted between 2011 and 2018 in Xinjiang, it shows how the rise of surveillance is linked to older, global histories of colonization and capitalism.

Silvia Lindtner's *Prototype Nation: China and the Contested Promise of Innovation* (Princeton University Press, 2020) examines the growth of high-tech development in China from the perspective of workers, designers and investors. This text is an important supplement to *In the Camps* that shows the global interlinkages, goals, and labor practices associated with the Chinese technology industry.

Geoffery Cain's *The Perfect Police State* (PublicAffairs, 2021) draws on interviews with Uyghurs in Turkey and the United States to understand the early effects of the surveillance systems.

Joanne Smith Finley's article "Securitization, Insecurity and Conflict in Contemporary Xinjiang: Has PRC Counter-terrorism Evolved into State Terror?" (*Central Asian Survey*, 2019) is an authoritative account of the rise of the camp system and its effects.

Sean Roberts's *The War on the Uyghurs: China's Internal Campaign Against a Muslim Minority* (Princeton University Press, 2020) examines state policy toward the Uyghurs and how Chinese policy is linked to the Global War on Terror. It provides a macro view of the systems described in this book.

James Millward's *Eurasian Crossroads: A History of Xinjiang* (Hurst Publishers, 2021) provides the most authoritative and up-to-date history of the region. It tells the history of the way Xinjiang became a penal colony.

Mamtimin Ala's *Worse Than Death: Reflections on the Uyghur Genocide* (Hamilton Books, 2021) presents deeply personal reflections on the effects of the camp system in Uyghur society. Written from the perspective of an Uyghur modernist philosopher, it attempts to articulate the inarticulable horror of watching a people be destroyed.

Lisa Ross's *Living Shrines of Uyghur China* (Monacelli Press, 2013) is a collection of portraits of Uyghur shrines and sacred landscapes. These beautiful images provide an evocative visual account of the Uyghur claims to their ancestral homeland. Since 2017, the Chinese state has erased the majority of these spaces.

Rian Thum's *The Sacred Routes of Uyghur History* (Harvard University Press, 2014) tells the living history of Uyghur collective memory. It demonstrates what is at stake in destroying the society of the Uyghur people.

Guldana Salimjan's "Mapping Loss, Remembering Ancestors: Genealogical Narratives of Kazakhs in China" (*Asian Ethnicity*, 2020) examines the stories told by Kazakh women to evoke the life histories of their ancestors and their attachment to the land of Northern Xinjiang. Salimjan, herself a native Kazakh from China, describes the way Kazakh women care for each other and the places they come from.

140 NOTES

INTRODUCTION

10 **7,700 such surveillance hubs:** Chun Han Wong, "China's Hard Edge: The Leader of Beijing's Muslim Crackdown Gains Influence," *Wall Street Journal*, April 7, 2019, https://www.wsj.com /articles/chinas-hard-edge-the -leader-of-beijings-muslim -crackdown-gains-influence -11554655886.

12 **security contractors hired:** "奎屯-独山子便民警务站公开招 聘协警公告Kuitun-Dushanzi Convenient Police Station Public Recruitment Announcement," Sohu .com, February 6, 2017, https:// www.sohu.com/a/125565427 _130552; I discuss the ninety thousand who were hired and their work in detail in chapter 3.

13 **China should "occupy" the region:** "Memorandum of Conversation Between Stalin and CCP Delegation, June 27, 1949," Wilson Center Digital Archive, https://digitalarchive.wilsoncenter .org/document/113380.pdf?v=a72a 4ae09caba5e4c7034a5c2eb69c0d.

14 **adapted to the cultural traditions:** James A. Millward, *Eurasian Crossroads: A History of Xinjiang* (Hurst Publishers, 2021), pp. 265–270.

14 **began to change in the 1990s:** Nicolas Becquelin, "Staged Development in Xinjiang," *China Quarterly* (2004), pp. 358–378.

15 **became tenant farmers:** Millward, *Eurasian Crossroads*.

15 **"crushed by the Chinese military":** Abduweli Ayup, *Mehbusluq Zawuti* [*The Prisoner Factory: A Memoir*] (Manuscript 2021), pp. 12-13.

16 **Uyghur student protest:** Darren Byler, "Requiem for the Living Dead Ten Years After 7-5," *SupChina*, July 3, 2019, https:// supchina.com/2019/07/03/requiem -for-the-living-dead-ten-years -after-7-5/.

16 **led to the disappearance:** Human Rights Watch, 2009, "'We Are Afraid to Even Look for Them': Enforced Disappearances in the Wake of Xinjiang's Protests," October 20, 2009, https://www .hrw.org/report/2009/10/20/we -are-afraid-even-look-them /enforced-disappearances-wake -xinjiangs-protests.

16 **Sean Roberts and Gardner Bovingdon have shown:** Sean Roberts, *The War on the Uyghurs: China's Internal Campaign Against a Muslim Minority* (Princeton University Press, 2020); Gardner Bovingdon, *The Uyghurs: Strangers in Their Own Land* (Columbia University Press, 2010).

18 **ten thousand Uyghurs fled to Turkey:** Sean Roberts, *The War on the Uyghurs*.

18   venomous snakes and disease-carrying insects: Darren Byler, "Imagining Re-Engineered Uyghurs in Northwest China," *Milestones: Commentary on the Islamic World,* April 20, 2017, https://www.milestonesjournal.net/photo-essays/2017/4/20/imagining-re-engineered-muslims-in-northwest-china.

19   rivaled East Germany: Adrian Zenz and James Leibold, "Securitizing Xinjiang: Police Recruitment, Informal Policing and Ethnic Minority Co-optation," *China Quarterly* 242 (2020), pp. 324–348; John O. Koehler, *Stasi: The Untold Story of the East German Secret Police* (Westview Press, 1999).

19   10 to 20 percent: James Leibold, "The Spectre of Insecurity: The CCP's Mass Internment Strategy in Xinjiang," *China Leadership Monitor,* March 1, 2019, https://www.prcleader.org/leibold. These findings are consistent with internal police documents from numerous locations across Xinjiang (Ürümchi, Aksu, Qaraqash) and estimates of capacity of detention facilities when correlated with former detainee interviews.

19   drop in birth rates: "新疆地区人口变动情况分析报告Analysis Report on Population Changes in Xinjiang," Xinjiang Development Research Center, January 7, 2021, https://t.co/J7WBkkousI?amp=1.

20   Meiya Pico or FiberHome: Megha Rajagopalan, "China Is Forcing People to Download an App That Tells Them to Delete 'Dangerous' Photos," *Buzzfeed,* April 9, 2018, https://www.buzzfeednews.com/article/meghara/china-surveillance-app; Raymond Zhong, "China Snares Tourists' Phones in Surveillance Dragnet by Adding Secret App," *New York Times,* July 2, 2019, https://www.nytimes.com/2019/07/02/technology/china-xinjiang-app.html.

20   accused of in a public statement: "Scholars Spreading Rumors About Uyghur Detention Work for US Intel Agency: Spokesperson," *Global Times,* December 3, 2019, https://www.globaltimes.cn/content/1172046.shtml.

21   did not rise to the level of criminality: "Information Received from China on Follow-up to the Concluding Observations on its Combined Fourteenth to Seventeenth Periodic Reports," United Nations, October 8, 2019, https://undocs.org/CERD/C/CHN/FCO/14-17.

21   a manual used by state workers: "The 'Four Togethers' and 'Three Gifts' Handbook," Chinese Ministry of Civil Affairs, https://xinjiang.sppga.ubc.ca/policy-documents/government-sources/cadre-materials/the-four

142   -togethers-and-three-gifts
-handbook/.

21   "more than two hundred
times": "Xiheba Precinct Risk
Evaluation Judgment Report
During Ramadan 2018," Xinjiang
Ministry of Public Security,
translated by the *Intercept*,
https://www.documentcloud
.org/documents/20466261
-document-24.

21   over three hundred camps:
"The Xinjiang Data Project,"
Australia Strategic Policy Institute,
2020, https://xjdp.aspi.org.au/.

22   533,000 were formally
prosecuted: Xinjiang People's
Procuratorate Annual Work
Reports 2018–2021; Supreme
People's Procuratorate Annual
Work Reports 2018–2021

22   higher than 99 percent:
Donald Clarke, "China's low
acquittal rates: interesting
statistics," *The China Collection*, May
5, 2020, https://thechinacollection
.org/chinas-low-acquittal-rates
-interesting-statistics/.

23   diplomatic exchange:
"Countering the Root Causes of
violent Extremism Undermining
Growth and Stability in China's
Xinjiang Region by Sharing UK Best
Practice," United Kingdom, Foreign,
Commonwealth and Development
Office, March 31, 2017, https://
devtracker.fcdo.gov.uk/projects
/GB-GOV-3-PAP-CNF-002340.

23   As many as five hundred
thousand children: Amy Qin, "In
China's Crackdown on Muslims,
Children Have Not Been Spared,"
New York Times, October 15, 2020,
https://www.nytimes.com/2019
/12/28/world/asia/china-xinjiang
-children-boarding-schools.html.

CHAPTER ONE

26   Implemented in her
hometown: "奎屯市召开网络安
全和信息化工作推进会Kuitun
City holds a network security
and informationization work
promotion meeting," *Kuitun Zero
Distance*, January 20, 2017, https://
archive.fo/tWk0l.

26   "pre-criminals," as state
authorities referred to them:
United Nations, 2019.

26   "round up everyone who
should be rounded up": Austin
Ramzy and Chris Buckley,
"'Absolutely No Mercy': Leaked
Files Expose How China Organized
Mass Detentions of Muslims,"
New York Times, November 16,
2019, https://www.nytimes.com
/interactive/2019/11/16/world/asia
/china-xinjiang-documents.html.

28   "sheer luck": Primo Levi,
Survival in Auschwitz (Simon &
Schuster, 1996).

29   centralized controlled
education training center:
"'Eradicating Ideological Viruses':
China's Campaign of Repression

Against Xinjiang's Muslims," Human Rights Watch, September 9, 2018, https://www.hrw.org/report /2018/09/09/eradicating -ideological-viruses/chinas -campaign-repression-against -xinjiangs.

30 **camera and audio recording system:** This is likely a system similar to Lonbon smart prisons, which are widely used in Xinjiang. See Darren Byler, "The Global Implications of 'Re-education' Technologies in Northwest China," Center for Global Policy, 2020, https://cgpolicy.org/articles /the-global-implications-of -re-education-technologies-in -northwest-china/.

30 **new wing . . . was completed:** This addition is clearly visible over this period in the satellite imagery of the camp location at these coordinates: 44.412373, 85.070769; See Shawn Zhang, "Satellite Imagery of Xinjiang Re-education Camp no. 81," May 18, 2019, https:// medium.com/@shawnwzhang /satellite-imagery-of-xinjiang-re -education-camp-81-28432a89b05.

31 **more than 10 percent of the total adult population:** *Xinjiang Statistical Yearbook* (China Statistics Press, 2018).

33 **used by Chinese state authorities to describe prohibitions:** Zhu Hailun, "Opinions on Further Strengthening and Standardizing

Vocational Skills Education and Training Centers Work," Autonomous Region State Organ Telegram: New Party Politics and Law, No. 419, 2017, https://www .documentcloud.org/documents /6558510-China-Cables-Telegram -English.html#text/p1.

34 **online behavior could be detected:** "新疆一男子被拘留15天，只因他在朋友圈说了这些话 . . . A man in Xinjiang was detained for fifteen days because he said these things in the circle of friends," Beijiang Broadcasting, August 2, 2019, https://archive.fo/I4gSg.

34 **"spread positive energy":** Darren Byler, "Sealed Doors and Positive Energy," *SupChina*, March 4, 2020, https://supchina.com /2020/03/04/sealed-doors-and -positive-energy-covid-19-in -xinjiang/.

35 **an immense dataset:** "China: Minority Region Collects DNA from Millions," Human Rights Watch, December 13, 2017, https:// www.hrw.org/news/2017/12/13 /china-minority-region-collects -dna-millions.

CHAPTER TWO

39 **viral sensation on the nascent Uyghur internet:** Rachel Harris and Aziz Isa, "'Invitation to a Mourning Ceremony': Perspectives on the Uyghur Internet," *Inner Asia* (2011), pp. 27–49.

144   40   **partially outside of the censorship capacities:** Darren Byler, "I Researched Uighur Society in China for Eight Years and Watched How Technology Opened New Opportunities—Then Became a Trap," *The Conversation,* September 18, 2019, https:// theconversation.com/i-researched -uighur-society-in-china-for -8-years-and-watched-how -technology-opened-new -opportunities-then-became-a -trap-119615.

40   **who began to study Islam by smartphone:** Rachel Harris and Aziz Isa, "Islam by Smartphone: Reading the Uyghur Islamic Revival on WeChat," *Central Asian Survey* 38, no. 1 (2019), pp. 61–80.

41   **"China's 9/11":** Jonathan Kaiman and Tania Branigan, "Kunming Knife Attack: Xinjiang Separatists Blamed for 'Chinese 9/11,'" *Guardian,* March 2, 2014, https://www.theguardian.com /world/2014/mar/02/kunming -knife-attack-muslim-separatists -xinjiang-china.

42   **a process of "Talibanization":** Darren Byler, "Ghost World,*" Logic* magazine, May 1, 2019, https://logicmag.io /china/ghost-world/.

42   **"People's War on Terror":** Timothy Grose, "Once Their Mental State Is Healthy, They Will Be Able to Live Happily in Society," *ChinaFile,* August 2, 2019, http://

www.chinafile.com/reporting -opinion/viewpoint/once-their -mental-state-healthy-they-will -be-able-live-happily-society.

42   **techniques of counterinsurgency:** Darren Byler, "Preventative Policing as Community Detention in Northwest China," *Made in China Journal,* October 25, 2019, https:// madeinchinajournal.com/2019 /10/25/preventative-policing -as-community-detention-in -northwest-china/.

42   **seventy-five official signs of Islamic extremism:** "Learning and Identifying 75 Religious Extreme Activities in Parts of Xinjiang," United Front Department, Communist Party of China, Translated by Darren Byler, https://xinjiang.sppga.ubc.ca /policy-documents/government -sources/online-sources /identifying-religious-extremism/.

43   **contractors such as Palantir:** "曹巍组团四大超炫硬科技CEO，解锁软着陆是能力还是态度|蓝驰论坛 Cao Wei asks four super cool cutting-edge technology CEOs to discuss whether achieving a soft landing comes from ability or attitude," Lanchi Forum, August 28, 2017, https://bit.ly/2Rp8G84.

43   **more than 50 percent of the industry:** "鸟瞰人工智能市场A Bird's Eye View of the Artificial Intelligence Market," Yi Ou Intelligence, September 2017,

https://web.archive.org/web
/20200820001947/http://img1
.iyiou.com/ThinkTank/2017
/HowAIBoostsUpSecurity
IndustryV6.pdf.

44 **in Xinjiang the state awarded:**
"Banking Body Prepares List of PPP
Projects in Xinjiang," *China Daily,*
February 24, 2017, https://archive.
fo/qWS04. See also Joshua Chin
and Liza Lin, *Surveillance State:
Inside China's Quest to Launch a New
Era of Social Control* (St. Martin's
Press, 2021).

44 **one of the largest receivers
of capital:** "新疆216个PPP项目落
地落地 项目数居全国第二位With
216 PPP Projects in Xinjiang Is the
Second Largest in the Country,"
People's Daily, November 14, 2017,
https://web.archive.org/web/
20210428213003/http://www
.csjrw.cn/2017/1114/72190.shtml;
Ben Dooley, "Chinese Firms Cash in
on Xinjiang's Growing Police State,"
AFP, June 27, 2018, https://www
.afp.com/en/chinese-firms-cash
-xinjiangs-growing-police-state.

44 **building of detention
facilities and related
infrastructure:** "关于2017年
自治区预算执行情况和2018年
自治区预算草案的报告Report
on the Implementation of the
Autonomous Region's budget in
2017 and the Draft Budget of the
Autonomous Region in 2018,"
Autonomous Region Department
of Finance, February 3, 2018,
https://web.archive.org/web

/20180312143344/http://www
.xinjiangnet.com.cn/2018/0203
/2044552.shtml.

44 **new tools in the region's
surveillance system:** "新疆安
防市场爆发，业绩拐点已现 The
Breakout of the Xinjiang Security
Market, and Its Performance
Turning Point Revealed," Sinolink
Securities, March 12, 2018, https://
web.archive.org/web/2020041911
0824/http://pdf.dfcfw.com/pdf
/H3_AP201803131102971114_1.pdf.

44 **1,400 private firms
competing for lucrative contracts:**
James Millward and Dahlia
Peterson, "China's System of
Oppression in Xinjiang: How It
Developed and How to Curb It,"
Brookings Institute, September
2020, https://www.brookings.edu
/research/chinas-system-of
-oppression-in-xinjiang-how-it
-developed-and-how-to-curb-it/.

44 **state capital investment
in data-intensive technologies:**
Martin Beraja, David Y. Yang, and
Noam Yuchtman, "Data-Intensive
Innovation and the State: Evidence
from AI Firms in China," NBER
Working Paper No. w27723, 2020,
https://economics.mit.edu/files
/19807.

45 **offered rewards of around
\$300 per criminal conviction:** "新
疆喀什警方开通网上暴恐视频信
息举报平台Xinjiang Kashgar Police
Opens Online Violent Terrorism
Reporting Platform," *China News*

146 *Network,* September 15, 2014, https://archive.vn/be7Va.

45 human-to-human citizen policing: "新疆查处多起传播暴恐音视频、宗教极端思想案违法信息案例Xinjiang Investigated and Dealt with Multiple Cases of Illegal Information Dissemination of Violent and Terrorist Audio and Video, Religious Extremism," *Xinjiang Daily,* April 17, 2017, http://www.myzaker.com/article/58f45a801bc8e07034000001/.

46 Ilham Tohti: Darren Byler, "Ilham Tohti's Sakharov Prize and the Desecration of Uyghur Society," *SupChina,* November 6, 2019, https://supchina.com/2019/11/06/ilham-tohtis-sakharov-prize-and-the-desecration-of-uyghur-society/.

48 digital enclosure is not exclusive: Mark Andrejevic, "Surveillance in the Digital Enclosure," *Communication Review* 10, no. 4 (2007), pp. 295–317.

49 data doors at the checkpoints: "China's Algorithms of Repression," Human Rights Watch, May 1, 2019, https://www.hrw.org/report/2019/05/01/chinas-algorithms-repression/reverse-engineering-xinjiang-police-mass-surveillance.

49 leading camera and face recognition companies: Darren Byler, "The Global Implications of 'Re-education' Technologies in Northwest China," Center for Global Policy, 2020, https://cgpolicy.org/articles/the-global-implications-of-re-education-technologies-in-northwest-china/.

49 "safe city" system: "Xinjiang Shawan County Smart (Safe) Project Feasibility Study," Chinese Government Procurement Network, 2017, p. 10. Hosted at https://www.chinafile.com/library/reports/xinjiang-shawan-county-smart-safe-project-feasibility-study.

50 similar to Clearview AI: Ryan Mac, "Clearview's Facial Recognition App Has Been Used by the Justice Department, ICE, Macy's, Walmart, and the NBA," *Buzzfeed,* February 27, 2020, https://www.buzzfeednews.com/article/ryanmac/clearview-ai-fbi-ice-global-law-enforcement.

50 project in London: Sean Gallagher, "London to Deploy Live Facial Recognition to Find Wanted Faces in a Crowd," arsTechnica, January 28, 2020, https://arstechnica.com/information-technology/2020/01/london-to-deploy-live-facial-recognition-to-find-wanted-faces-in-crowd/.

51 submitted their biometric data: Sui-Lee Wee, "China Uses DNA to Track Its People, with the Help of American Expertise," *New York Times*, February 21, 2019, https://www.nytimes.com/2019

/02/21/business/china-xinjiang -uighur-dna-thermo-fisher.html.

51   in 0.8 seconds it can run a match of a face: "Xinjiang Shawan County Smart (Safe) City Project Feasibility Study," p. 89.

51   smartphone-driven digital model: "着力打造'最亲民'服务窗口 Efforts to create the 'closest to the people' service window," *Worker Times*, May 24, 2019, http://archive .fo/mPF40.

51   scan the applicant's face: "新 疆户籍居民身份证丢失补领可网上 自助办理了！附操作指南Replacing lost or reissuing Xinjiang resident ID card can be done online! Use this self-service operation guide," Shawan County Public Security Bureau, October 12, 2018, http:// archive.vn/a6Rhm.

51   social security benefits: "戳一 下，请了解"新疆智慧人社"APP待遇 领取资格认证详细操作流程Check this, please understand in detail how the operation process of the 'Xinjiang Smart Human Society' APP qualification certification will be treated," Shawan County Human Resources and Social Security Bureau, 2018, http://archive.fo /lbdnK.

51   pass through neighborhood checkpoints: "好消息！沙湾 这8个小区正式实行人脸识别门 禁系统啦！Good news! The 8 Neighborhood Watch Units in Shawan have officially implemented

a face recognition access control system!" Shawan Golden Shield, 2018, http://archive.fo/Ha01B.

51   rural farmer work brigades: "沙湾县：合作社拓宽致富路 小 农户迈向大农业Shawan County: Brigades broaden Zhifu Road and small farmers are moving toward large-scale agriculture," Shawan Zero Distance, December 14, 2018, http://archive.fo/aX1VS.

52   "data janitors": Lilly Irani, "Justice for Data Janitors," Public Books, January 15, 2015, https:// www.publicbooks.org/justice -for-data-janitors/.

52   ninety thousand police contractors: Adrian Zenz and James Leibold, "Securitizing Xinjiang: Police Recruitment, Informal Policing and Ethnic Minority Co-optation," *China Quarterly* 242 (2020), pp. 324–348.

52   basic qualification for the job": 沙湾县公安局招聘100名事业 编制便民警务站工作人员Shawan County Public Security Bureau Recruits 100 Staff Members to Work in the People's Convenience Police Stations," Peaceful Shawan, August 22, 2017, http://archive.fo /sjWJJ.

53   regionwide process of checking people's devices: Darren Byler, "Chinese Infrastructures of Population Management on the New Silk Road," Wilson International Center for Scholars, 2021.

148

53 sent names of "pushes":
Yael Grauer, "Revealed: Massive
Chinese Police Database,"
Intercept, January 29, 2021, https://
theintercept.com/2021/01/29
/china-uyghur-muslim
-surveillance-police/.

**53 patterns of suspicious
behaviors:** "China's Algorithms of
Repression," Human Rights Watch,
May 1, 2019, https://www.hrw.org
/report/2019/05/01/chinas
-algorithms-repression/reverse
-engineering-xinjiang-police
-mass-surveillance.

53 "race-as-algorithm":
Sareeta Amrute, "Bored Techies
Being Casually Racist: Race as
Algorithm," *Science, Technology
& Human Values,* 45, 5 (2020): pp.
903–933.

**54 "considered very well
qualified":** "Сұмдық СҰХБАТ
Terrifying Interview," Atajurt
Kazakh Human Rights, January 11,
2019, https://www.youtube.com
/watch?v=p8rVTEStmY8.

54 Hua Chenzu: "援疆干部风采
录A Record of the Cadres Who 'Aid
Xinjiang,'" Changji Public Security
Bureau, December 25, 2019, https://
archive.vn/tFO2N.

55 seventy-seven stations": 沙湾
县公安局招聘100名事业编制便民警
务站工作人员Shawan County Public
Security Bureau Recruits 100 Staff
Members to Work in the People's

Convenience Police Stations,"
Peaceful Shawan, August 22, 2017,
http://archive.fo/sjWJJ.

**58 "centralized closed education
training center":** Shawn Zhang,
"Satellite Imagery of Xinjiang
Re-education Camp no. 83," May 18,
2019, https://medium
.com/@shawnwzhang/satellite
-imagery-of-xinjiang-re-education
-camp-83-377e9453db7a.

**58 more than a hundred
testimonies:** "Victims by County
of Origin," Xinjiang Victims
Database, 2021, https://shahit.biz
/eng/#map.

**59 "The indirect economic
benefits are immeasurable":**
"Xinjiang Shawan County Smart
(Safe) Project Feasibility Study, "
Chinese Government Procurement
Network, 2017, pp. 6, 183. Hosted at
https://www.chinafile.com/library
/reports/xinjiang-shawan-county
-smart-safe-project-feasibility
-study.

59 Xue Bing: "2017年4月24号沙
湾新闻Shawan News on April 24,
2017," *Shawan News,* April 24, 2017,
http://archive.fo/bhPnC.

CHAPTER THREE

**65 four-story building
surrounded by razor wire:**
"Saybagh Facility #1," Xinjiang Data
Project, 2021, https://xjdp.aspi.org
.au/map/?marker=3298.

70 **"what gives violence its power and meaning"**: Nancy Scheper-Hughes and Philippe Bourgois (eds.), *Violence in War and Peace: An Anthology* (Blackwell, 2004).

71 **"what they represent"**: Didier Fassin, *Enforcing Order: An Ethnography of Urban Policing* (Polity, 2013), p. 7.

71 **those who have been deemed "untrustworthy"**: Joanne Smith Finley, "Securitization, Insecurity and Conflict in Contemporary Xinjiang: Has PRC Counter-terrorism Evolved into State Terror?" *Central Asian Survey* 38, no. 1 (2019), pp. 1–26.

72 **"new IUD that state workers had forced her to implant"**: 关于印发《古牧地镇2019年违法生育"两个彻查"专项行动实施方案》的通知 Notice on Printing and Distributing the 'Implementation Plan for the "Two Thorough Investigations" of Special Actions for Illegal Childbirth in Gumudi Town in 2019,'" Midong District Government, July 21, 2019, https://archive.vn/iGaGS; Qelbinur describes the forced implantation of her IUD in Emma Graham-Harrison and Lily Kuo, "Uighur Muslim Teacher Tells of Forced Sterilisation in Xinjiang," *Guardian,* September 4, 2020, https://www.theguardian.com/world/2020/sep/04/muslim-minority-teacher-50-tells-of-forced-sterilisation-in-xinjiang-china.

72 **would not be added to the list of "trustworthy" citizens:** "《哈巴河县持续深入开展违法生育专项治理工作实施方案》政策解读Policy Interpretation of the 'Implementation Plan for Habahe County to Continue and Intensify the Special Treatment of Illegal Childbirth,'" Habahe County Government, June 26, 2020, https://archive.fo/7wyhZ.

72 **"disposed of early"**: Policy Interpretation of the "Implementation Plan for Habahe County to Continue and Intensify the Special Treatment of Illegal Childbirth."

72 **to anyone who reported violations of family planning regulations:** "巡视公告；阿克苏市举报违反计划生育政策行为'两个彻查'的通告Announcement of Inspection; Notice of 'Two thorough investigations' on Reporting Violations of Family Planning Policies in Aksu City," Aksu City Zero Distance, May 11, 2019, https://archive.is/C97TN.

72 **as many as 10 percent of all detainees:** "The Qaraqash List," Qaraqash Public Security Bureau, 2018, hosted at https://shahit.biz/supp/list_008.pdf; see also Gene Bunin, "The Elephant in the XUAR: III," *Living Otherwise,* April 2021, https://livingotherwise.com/wp-content/uploads/2021/04

150 /Elephant-in-the-XUAR-III.
-Gene-A.-Bunin.pdf.

73 plummeted by between 50 and 80 percent: Li Xiaoxia, "新疆地区人口变动情况分析报告Analysis Report on Population Changes in Xinjiang," Xinjiang Development Research Center, 2021, http://archive.is/O1vOg; Sigal Samuel, "China's Genocide Against the Uyghurs, in 4 Disturbing Charts," Vox, March 10, 2021, https://www.vox.com/future-perfect/22311356/china-uyghur-birthrate-sterilization-genocide.

74 "terrorists must be everywhere": Darren Byler, "'The Atmosphere Has Become Abnormal': Han Chinese Views from Xinjiang," SupChina, November 4, 2020, https://supchina.com/2020/11/04/han-chinese-views-from-xinjiang/.

74 her relatives complained about the checkpoints: Darren Byler, "'Uyghurs Are So Bad': Chinese Dinner Table Politics in Xinjiang," SupChina, June 3, 2020, https://supchina.com/2020/06/03/uyghurs-are-so-bad-chinese-dinner-table-politics-in-xinjiang/.

75 what it meant to be a good citizen Darren Byler, "China's Government Has Ordered a Million Citizens to Occupy Uighur Homes. Here's What They Think They're Doing," ChinaFile, October 24, 2018,

https://www.chinafile.com/reporting-opinion/postcard/million-citizens-occupy-uighur-homes-xinjiang.

76 From the razor wire and automatic weapons: For more on the history of technology in camp systems, see Andrea Pitzer, One Long Night: A Global History of Concentration Camps, Little, Brown, and Company, 2017.

76 normalizing relationships of domination in more and more intimate ways: Ann Laura Stoler, Carnal Knowledge and Imperial Power: Race and the Intimate in Colonial Rule (University of California Press, 2010).

77 the internal directives from the head of security: Zhu Hailun, "Opinions on Further Strengthening and Standardizing Vocational Skills Education and Training Centers Work," Autonomous Region State Organ Telegram: New Party Politics and Law, No. 419, 2017, https://www.documentcloud.org/documents/6558510-China-Cables-Telegram-English.html#text/p1.

79 the command center of a "smart camp" system: "大华专业行业智慧营区方案Dahua Professional Industry Smart Camp Project," Dahua Technology Co., Ltd., https://archive.fo/cmqVs; "航天华拓实力助攻新疆某营区信息化建设Aerospace Huatuo's Strength

Assists in the Informatization Construction of a Camp in Xinjiang," Aerospace Huatuo Technology Co., Ltd. Oct. 2019, https://archive.fo/EO1ix.

79 **"perfect peripheral isolation":** Zhu Hailun, "Opinions on Further Strengthening and Standardizing Vocational Skills Education and Training Centers Work."

79 **"be defended like a prison":** Ben Dooley, "Inside China's Internment Camps," *AFP,* October 25, 2018, https://www.afp.com/en/inside-chinas-internment-camps-tear-gas-tasers-and-textbooks.

79 **"emotion or affect recognition":** "来邦监仓可视对讲系统 在新疆七所监狱中标！The Video Intercom System of LonBon Won the Bid in Seven Prisons in Xinjiang!" LonBon, November 21, 2017, http://archive.fo/571tE.

80 **"eliminate the ideological problems of prisoners":** "智慧监狱系统开发解决方案，新疆智慧监所可视化系统平台建设 The smart prison system development solution, construction of the visualization platform of the Xinjiang Smart Prison," Yuanzhong Ruiwu, April 13, 2021, https://archive.fo/pSgA0. For more on the use of affect recognition in Xinjiang detention facilities, see, Jane Wakefield, "AI emotion-detection software tested on Uyghurs," BBC, May 26, 2021,

https://www.bbc.com/news/technology-57101248.   151

81 **threat of being labeled "two faced":** Memtimin Ala, "Turn in the Two-Faced: The Plight of Uyghur Intellectuals," *Diplomat*, October 12, 2018, https://thediplomat.com/2018/10/turn-in-the-two-faced-the-plight-of-uyghur-intellectuals/.

82 **"Look, a Negro!":** Frantz Fanon, *Black Skin, White Masks* (Grove Press, 1967).

83 **to remain forever stuck in forms of mimicry:** Homi Bhabha, *The Location of Culture* (Routledge, 2012).

CHAPTER FOUR

91 **"as cart-drivers do":** Primo Levi, *Survival in Auschwitz*, p. 67.

92 **"because you are not humans":** "Ihr seid keine Menschen," *Die Zeit*, 2019, https://www.zeit.de/2019/32/zwangslager-xinjiang-muslimechina-zeugen-menschenrechte/seite-2.

92 **rats that needed to be chased and "beaten down":** "习近平:要使暴力恐怖分子成为'过街老鼠 人人喊打' Xi Jinping: Turn the Violent Terrorists into, "Rats Running Through the Street, While Everyone Beats Them Down,'" *Xinhua News,* April 26, 2014, https://archive.fo/JJ2LQ.

93 **"I only thought about food":** *Die Zeit*, 2019.

97 **the smell of the hundreds of detainees he helped to round up each day:** "信阳市看守所开展'学习十九大 弘扬援疆精神'专题活动Xinyang City Detention Center Launches the Special Activity of 'Learning from the 19th CPC National Congress and Carrying Forward the Spirit of Aid Xinjiang,'" Xinyang City Detention Center, December 23, 2017, https://archive.vn/Etdjz.

97 **a converted nursing home:** "Shihu Facility #6," Xinjiang Data Project, 2021, https://xjdp.aspi.org.au/map/?marker=3541.

99 **so that they could hide any other "abnormal deaths":** Zhu Hailun, "Opinions on Further Strengthening and Standardizing Vocational Skills Education and Training Centers Work."

100 **as many as 70 percent of children:** *Xinjiang Statistical Yearbook* (China Statistics Press, 2018). See also Adrian Zenz, "Break Their Roots: Evidence for China's Parent-Child Separation Campaign in Xinjiang," *Journal of Political Risk* 7, no. 7 (July 4, 2019), https://www.jpolrisk.com/break-their-roots-evidence-for-chinas-parent-child-separation-campaign-in-xinjiang/.

102 **"the problem of the remote future has grown pale":** Primo Levi, *Survival in Auschwitz*, p. 36.

CHAPTER FIVE

104 **shared some religious videos:** Ben Mauk, "Inside China's Prison State," *New Yorker,* February 2021, https://www.newyorker.com/news/a-reporter-at-large/china-xinjiang-prison-state-uighur-detention-camps-prisoner-testimony.

108 **fifteen months of horrific abuse:** Erkin Azat, "Gulzira Auelkhan's Records in a Chinese Concentration Camp: 'I Worry About the Lives of Those Eight Who Have Not Signed a Contract in the Factory,'" *Medium*, March 4, 2019, medium.com/@erkinazat2018/gulzira-auelkhan-s-records-in-a-chinese-concentration-camp-i-worry-about-the-lives-of-those-c18a2038a5a2.

109 **had not actually committed a crime:** United Nations, 2019.

109 **Wang Xinghua:** "州直纺织服装产业敲开群众'就业门' The State Direct Textile and Garment Industry Knocks on 'Employment Door' of the Masses," Ili Television, December 4, 2018, archive.md/KSe5r.

110 **fewer than two hundred employees:** "Lixian Huawei Gloves Factory," Alibaba, 2019, https://web.archive.org/web/20191211094113/huaweiglove.en.alibaba.com/company_profile.html?spm=a2700.icbuShop.conu5cff17.1.4af811a5izQHdr.

110 **4 percent of new factory's sales volume was subsidized:** "关于进一步完善自治区纺织服装产业 政策的通知 Notice on Further Improving the Textile and Apparel Industry Policy of the Autonomous Region," Government of the Xinjiang Uyghur Autonomous Region, April 6, 2018, archive.fo/ZBsk8.

110 **a "carrier" of economic stability:** "自治区经济结构稳中有活发展良好 The Economic Structure of the Autonomous Region Is Stable, Alive and Well Developed," Xinjiang Reform and Development Commission, December 2018, web.archive.org/web/20190520143306/http:/www.xjdrc.gov.cn/info/9923/23516.htm.

110 **sources more than 80 percent of its cotton:** "Provincial Data Shows China's Shifting Agricultural Trends," Gro Intelligence, March 6, 2019, gro-intelligence.com/insights/articles/provincial-data-shows-chinas-shifting-agricultural-trends.

111 **more than a million textile and garment industry jobs:** Dominique Patton, "Xinjiang Cotton at Crossroads of China's New Silk Road," Reuters, January 12, 2016, www.reuters.com/article/us-china-xinjiang-cotton-insight-idUSKCN0UQ00320160112.

111 **one in every eleven:** "Wages and Working Hours in the Textiles, Clothing, Leather and Footwear Industries," International Labor Organisation, 2014, www.ilo.org/wcmsp5/groups/public/@ed_dialogue/@sector/documents/publication/wcms_300463.pdf.

112 **a sign of untrustworthiness and religious extremism:** "Çin'in Yeni Planlarinin Yazili Emri İfşa Oldu Written Order of China's New Plans Revealed," Turkistan Press, July 23, 2018, turkistanpress.com/page/cin-39-in-yeni-planlarinin-yazili-emri-ifsa-oldu/247; "Learning and Identifying 75 Religious Extreme Activities in Parts of Xinjiang," United Front Department, Communist Party of China, 2017, Translated by Darren Byler, https://xinjiang.sppga.ubc.ca/policy-documents/government-sources/online-sources/identifying-religious-extremism/.

113 **1,800 others were sent to work:** "伊宁县'轻纺产业区'的产业工人：幸福是奋斗出来的！ Industrial Workers in the 'Textile Industry Zone' of Yining County: Happiness Comes from Struggle!" Yining Zero Distance Yining, 2017, archive.md/Cv6w5 - selection-23.14-31.7.

113 **only sew thirteen pairs:** Nathan Vanderklippe, "'I Felt like a Slave': Inside China's Complex System of Incarceration and Control of Minorities," *Globe and Mail*, March 31, 2018, www.theglobeandmail.com/world/article-i-felt-like-a-slave-inside-chinas-complex-system-of-incarceration.

154

113 **"it was like slavery":** "Gulzira Aeulkhan," Xinjiang Victims Database, 2019, shahit.biz /eng/viewentry.php?entryno =1723.

115 **"watched at night by an official":** Nathan Vanderklippe, "'I Felt Like a Slave.'"

115 **"earning 300 yuan in total":** *Die Zeit*, 2019.

115 **100,000 detainees were scheduled to move to work:** "关于印发《喀什地区困难群体就业培训工作实施方案》的通知 Notice on Issuing the 'Implementation Plan for Employment Training for Disadvantaged Groups in Kashgar,'" Kashgar Regional Office, August 10, 2018, web.archive.org/web /20181204024839/http:/kashi.gov .cn/Government/PublicInfoShow .aspx?ID=2963.

115 **drawn from a population of around 45,000 total Muslims:** "2019年12月20号沙湾新闻 Shawan News for December 20, 2019," *Shawan News*, December 20, 2019, http://archive.fo/O8J0T.

117 **between $1.50 and $24.00 per pair:** Alibaba, 2019.

117 **"took off their grass shoes":** "Industrial Workers in the 'Textile Industry Zone' of Yining County: Happiness Comes from Struggle!"

117 **did not even pause to look up:** "The State Direct Textile and Garment Industry Knocks on 'Employment Door' of the Masses."

119 **threatened Gulzira in order to get her to sign:** Gene Bunin, "Detainees Are Trickling Out of the Camps," *Foreign Policy*, January 18, 2019, foreignpolicy.com/2019/01 /18/detainees-are-trickling-out -of-xinjiangs-camps.

120 **"whose coercion was maximal":** Primo Levi, *The Drowned and the Saved* (Vintage International Edition, 1989), p. 41.

121 **the "gray zone":** Primo Levi, *The Drowned and the Saved*.

CONCLUSION

123 **face recognition dataset:** "People Who Downloaded the MegaFace Face Recognition Dataset via FOIA Release from the University of Washington," no date, https://docs.google.com /spreadsheets/d/1Pg_Lg8OfqloNtny YaLyxAzYHEKYSJh1i3w500O1PCv Y/edit#gid=0; "UW CSE's MegaFace Challenge Shows Bigger Is Better for Facial Recognition," Paul G. Allen School of Computer Science and Engineering, June 23, 2016, https:// news.cs.washington.edu/2016/06 /23/uw-cses-megaface-challenge -shows-bigger-is-better-for -facial-recognition/.

123–24 **automated tools for ecommerce:** "一文读懂人脸识别技术 One Article to Understand Face Recognition Technology," AVIC

Web, June 25, 2019, https://archive
.fo/kI1Nw#selection-649.353
-649.365.

124   "in-depth partnerships":
"人工智能成城市发展新动能 旷视
科技Face++助力多地构建'城市大
脑'Artificial intelligence becomes
a new driving force for urban
development. Megvii Technology
Face++ helps build 'urban brains' in
many places," *Xinhua,* December 21,
2017, http://archive.fo/msIhN.

**124   Ministry of State Security
database:** "Alibaba-backed AI
Startup Megvii Weighing IPO This
Year: Sources," *Business Times,*
January 11, 2019, https://www
.businesstimes.com.sg/garage
/news/alibaba-backed-ai-startup
-megvii-weighing-ipo-this-year
-sources.

**124   Kai-Fu Lee used his own
venture capital firm:** Aron Chen,
"Venture Capital Big Shot's Remark
on Ant and Megvii Sharing Data
Sparks Public Concern," Pingwest,
September 18, 2020, https://
en.pingwest.com/a/7770.

**124   Lee helped to broker an
investment:** "One Article to
Understand Face Recognition
Technology."

**124   Taobao ecommerce
platform:** "One Article to
Understand Face Recognition
Technology."

**124   a relationship that they
would later deny:** Aron Chen,

"Venture Capital Big Shot's Remark
on Ant and Megvii Sharing Data
Sparks Public Concern."

124   Jue Wang: "Jue Wang, PhD,"
no date, https://www.juew.org/.

124   Megvii Research USA:
"Megvii," no date, https://www
.yellowpages.com/redmond-wa
/mip/megvii-540945646.

**125   other young computer
scientists:** "Xue Bai," no date,
https://sites.google.com/view
/xuebai/home.

**125   the lack of fruit in the break
room:** "Megvii," Glassdoor, no date,
https://www.glassdoor.com
/ReviewsMegvii-Reviews-E976241
_P2.htm.

125   "It *was* Silicon Valley":
Xiaowei Wang, *Blockchain Chicken
Farm,* 2020, FSG Originals x Logic,
2020, p. 157.

**125   "cradle of Chinese artificial
intelligence":** "极智探索 创见未
来——写在微软亚洲研究院20周年
之际 Exploring Extreme Intelligence
to Create a Future—Written on
the 20th Anniversary of Microsoft
Research Asia," Microsoft Research
Asia, November 5, 2018, https://
www.msra.cn/zh-cn/news
/executivebylines/msra-20th
-anniversary.

**125   nearly all major US tech
firms:** Ken Glueck, "The Intercept's
Latest . . . Not Even Sure Where to
Start," *Oracle News Connect,* April

156   27, 2021, https://www.oracle.com
/news/announcement/blog/the
-intercepts-latest-2001-04-27/.

126   **first it collaborated with
Alibaba:** "人工智能肉搏战：商汤和
旷视们的商业化征途 Hand-to-hand
Combat with Artificial Intelligence:
The Commercialization Journey
of SenseTime and Megvii," 36
Krypton, April 8, 2018, https://
36kr.com/p/1722417102849.

126   **Megvii hired a director of
the military contractor:** "17 年资
历的安防老兵，在旷视 Face++ 的所
闻所感A 17-year Security Veteran
on What He Hears and Feels
About Megvii's Face++," *Leiphone*,
November 24, 2017, https://www.
leiphone.com/news/201711/5l4j5
Twclkbnm6iQ.html.

126   **"counter-terrorism"
business:** "用人工智能协助新疆长
治久安 旷视(Face++)亮相第四届亚欧
安博会Using Artificial Intelligence
to assist Xinjiang's Long-term
Peace and Security (Face++) Debut
at the 4th Asia-Europe Security
Expo," *China Net*, August 25, 2017,
https://archive.fo/2AGKH
#selection-315.59-315.114.

126   **"public security makes
profit":** Glassdoor, no date.

127   **"everyone seemed to be ten
years younger":** "旷视(Face++)孙
剑：创业公司里的研究之美Megvii's
Face++ Sun Jian: The Beauty of
Research in Startups," *Heart of the
Machine*, January 11, 2017, https://
archive.fo/CA6kN.

128   **on the one-month
anniversary:** Kilic Bugra Kanat,
"'War on Terror' as a Diversionary
Strategy: Personifying Minorities
as Terrorists in the People's
Republic of China," *Journal of
Muslim Minority Affairs* 32, no. 4
(2012), pp. 507–527.

128   **revised the past history:**
"'East Turkistan' Terrorist Forces
Cannot Get Away with Impunity,"
Information Office of State Council,
January 21, 2002, http://china.org
.cn/english/2002/Jan/25582.htm.

129   **added the phantom,
Pakistan-based East Turkestan
Islamic Party:** Chien-peng
Chung, "China's 'War on Terror':
September 11 and Uighur
Separatism," *Foreign Affairs*,
September 1, 2002, https://
t.co/RgDhpnVkFS?amp=1; Sean
Roberts, 2020.

129   **all of them Uyghur:** "Terror
List with Links to al-Qaeda
Unveiled," *China Daily*, December
16, 2003, https://web.archive.
org/web/20031217110119/http://
chinadaily.com.cn/en/doc/2003-12
/16/content_290658.htm.

129   **the Uyghurs were "terrified":**
Darren Byler, "Terrifying Uyghurs,"
Living Otherwise, December 17,
2015, https://t.co/GMVBRusuS6
?amp=1.

129   **racialized "bad Muslim"
slot:** David Brophy, "Good and
Bad Muslims in Xinjiang." Made

in China., July 9, 2019. https://
madeinchinajournal.com
/2019/07/09/good-and-bad
-muslims-in-xinjiang/.

129   **any activity by ethnoracial
others:** Emily Yeh, "On Terrorism
and the Politics of Naming, *Cultural
Anthropology Online,* April 8, 2012,
https://culanth.org/fieldsights
/on-terrorism-and-the-politics
-of-naming.

129   **an official technical support
unit:** Despite multiple sources
confirming their role as support
unit, Megvii now denies these
claims. See Danielle Cave et al.,
"Mapping China's Tech Giants,"
Australia Strategic Policy Institute,
2019, https://chinatechmap.aspi
.org.au/#/company/megvii.

129   **"thousands of illegal
fugitives were arrested":** *Xinhua,*
2017. In the context of China,
"counter-terrorism" refers
almost exclusively to policing of
Uyghurs and other ethno-racial
minorities. See Ryan Mac et al.,
"US Universities and Retirees Are
Funding the Technology Behind
China's Surveillance State,"
Buzzfeed, June 5, 2019, https://
www.buzzfeednews.com/article
/ryanmac/us-money-funding
-facial-recognition-sensetime
-megvii; in a statement
communicated through Ginny
Wilmerding, a former partner at
Brunswick Group, Megvii stated
that it has not developed "any

solutions targeting specific ethnic
groups."

130   **"just provide the
government the technology":**
Rob Schmitz, "Facial Recognition
in China Is Big Business as Local
Governments Boost Surveillance,"
NPR, April 3, 2018, https://www
.npr.org/sections/parallels/2018
/04/03/598012923/facial
-recognition-in-china-is-big
-business-as-local-governments
-boost-surveilla.

130   **"networks of 50,000 to
100,000 surveillance cameras":**
Kai Strittmatter, *We Have Been
Harmonized* (Old Street Publishing,
2019), p. 170.

130   **"we perceive information
such as your identity":** "曠視
Face++出席AI領域年度盛會：用
AI構建「五度」城市感知Megvii's
Face++ Attends an Annual Event
in the AI Field: Using AI to Build
'Five Degrees' of City Perception,"
Technology Express, March 2018,
http://archive.fo/dJwtw.

130   **Megvii spokespeople later
claimed were not true:** Center for
Global Policy, 2020.

131   **"acting contrary to the
foreign policy interests":**
"Addition of Certain Entities to
the Entity List," *US Department of
Commerce,* October 9, 2019, https://
s3.amazonaws.com/public
-inspection.federalregister.gov
/2019-22210.pdf

158

131   **When I published a report:** Center for Global Policy, 2020.

131   **made less than $2 million in Xinjiang:** "US Blacklist is Not Stopping Megvii from Seeking a Hong Kong IPO," Al Jazeera, November 19, 2019, https://www .aljazeera.com/ajimpact/blacklist -stopping-megvii-seeking-hong -kong-ipo-191119185927551.html.

132   **"76 fugitives had been captured":** "A 17-year Security Veteran on What He Hears and Feels About Megvii's Face++."

132   **an "Uyghur alarm" tool:** "Huawei / Megvii Uyghur Alarms," IPVM, December 8, 2020, https:// ipvm.com/reports/huawei -megvii-uygur.

132   **1,500 heat-mapping camera systems:** Krystal Hu and Jeffrey Dastin, "Exclusive: Amazon Turns to Chinese Firm on U.S. Blacklist to Meet Thermal Camera Needs," Reuters, April 29, 2020, https:// www.reuters.com/article/us -health-coronavirus-amazon -com-cameras/exclusive-amazon -turns-to-chinese-firm-on-u -s-blacklist-to-meet-thermal -camera-needs-idUSKBN22B1AL.

133   **more than 180 countries:** Kirsty Needham, "Special Report: COVID Opens New Doors for China's Gene Giant," Reuters, August 5, 2020, https://www .reuters.com/article/us-health -coronavirus-bgi-specialreport /special-report-covid-opens-new -doors-for-chinas-gene-giant -idUSKCN2511CE.

133   **bought $1.2 million worth of tests:** "CEO Tyler Nottberg Teams Up with Local Business Leaders to Buy 50,000 COVID-19 Test Kits," *US Engineering*, March 25, 2020, https://www.usengineering .com/2020/03/ceo-tyler-nottberg -teams-up-with-local-business -leaders-to-buy-50000-covid-19 -test-kits/; "BGI Helps Kansas City Community Scale Up COVID-19 Testing," BGI, March 30, 2020, https://www.bgi.com/us/company /news/bgi-helps-kansas-city -community-scale-up-covid-19 -testing/.

133   **Megvii also capitalized:** "Private Eye: Megvii Exec on Power of AI Amid Pandemic," *China Daily*, May 28, 2020, https://www .chinadaily.com.cn/a/202005/28 /WS5eceec41a310a8b241158f2c .html.

133   **airports in South Korea and the United Arab Emirates:** Sun Ye, "Chinese Tech Companies Rise to COVID-19 Challenge," CGTN, August 29, 2020, https://news .cgtn.com/news/2020-08-29 /Chinese-tech-companies-rise-to -COVID-19-challenge-TlBXFQzr TW/index.html.

133   **"humanitarian experimentation":** Sanjana

Varghese, "Borders Everywhere," *Real Life Magazine*, August 12, 2020, https://reallifemag.com/borders -everywhere/.

133 **Amazon's own role:** Drew Harwell, "Oregon Became a Testing Ground for Amazon's Facial-recognition Policing. But What if Rekognition Gets It Wrong?" *Washington Post,* April 30, 2019, https://www.washingtonpost .com/technology/2019/04/30 /amazons-facial-recognition -technology-is-supercharging -local-police/.

133 **"behind Manchester stands Mississippi":** Jason W. Moore, "The Capitalocene Part II: Accumulation by Appropriation and the Centrality of Unpaid Work /Energy," *Journal of Peasant Studies,* 2017.

134 **making clear that *they work*:** Cai Yineng, "On China's 'Color Codes' and Life After COVID-19," *Sixth Tone*, April 9, 2020, https:// www.sixthtone.com/news /1005452/on-chinas-color -codes-and-life-after-covid-19.

134 **democratic states like New Zealand and Canada:** Konstantin Richter, "How New Zealand Beat the Coronavirus," *Politico*, May 14, 2020, https://www.politico.eu /article/kiwis-vs-coronavirus -new-zealand-covid19-restrictions -rules/; Ian Bremmer, "The Best Global Responses to the COVID-19 Pandemic, 1 Year Later," *Time,* February 23, 2021, https://time .com/5851633/best-global -responses-covid-19/.

134 **surveillance systems support systemic racism:** Angelique Carson, "Surveillance as a tool for racism," *TechCrunch*, April 25, 2016, https://techcrunch.com /2016/04/25/surveillance-as-a -tool-for-racism/.

135 **algorithms to detect racial phenotypes:** Parmy Olson, "The Quiet Growth of Race Detection Software Sparks Concerns Over Bias," *Wall Street Journal,* August 14, 2020, https://www.wsj.com /articles/the-quiet-growth -of-race-detection-software -sparks-concerns-over-bias -11597378154.

Columbia Global Reports is a publishing imprint from Columbia University that commissions authors to do original on-site reporting around the globe on a wide range of issues. The resulting novella-length books offer new ways to look at and understand the world that can be read in a few hours. Most readers are curious and busy. Our books are for them.

Subscribe to Columbia Global Reports and get six books a year in the mail in advance of publication. globalreports.columbia.edu/subscribe